WOMAN AS EARTH MOTHER . . .

"One afternoon my four-year-old put on his white terry-cloth bathrobe and a pair of rubber boots. He was always inventing costumes. This time he said, 'Do I look like God?'

" 'You always look something like God to me,' I said honestly. Few things I say are quite that deeply honest.

" 'God also wears a crown,' Peter reflected, feeling his lack. I looked at his crown of golden curls and kept quiet. Then he cheerfully explained the costume.

" 'God puts on His rubber boots when He makes a flood.'

"C. S. Lewis once said that next to the blessed sacrament, your neighbor is the holiest object presented to your senses. My own feeling is that if my neighbor is a child, especially a child entrusted to my nurture, he is the holiest of all."

It is Kathryn Lindskoog's rare ability to observe day-to-day life with a view to eternity that makes ON MY WAY UP FROM EDEN a unique, not-to-be-missed experience.

On My Way Up From Eden

KATHRYN LINDSKOOG

David C. Cook Publishing Co.
ELGIN, ILLINOIS—WESTON, ONTARIO
LA HABRA, CALIFORNIA

ON MY WAY UP FROM EDEN (formerly *Up From Eden*)
Copyright © 1976 David C. Cook Publishing Co.
First printing: April, 1976
Second printing: May, 1977

All rights reserved. Except for brief excerpts for review purposes, no part of this book may be reproduced or used in any form or by any means—electronic or mechanical, including photocopying, recording, or information storage and retrieval systems—without written permission from the publisher.

David C. Cook Publishing Co., Elgin, IL 60120

Printed in the United States of America
Library of Congress Catalog Number: 75-4040

ISBN: 0-912692-63-4

*To my only sister
and to my
many other sisters*

CONTENTS

1 Woman as Moon Goddess   11
2 Woman as Earth Mother   31
3 Woman's Fertility Rights   49
4 Woman's Objection to Subjection   63
5 Woman's Roleplay   79
6 Woman's Power Play   99
7 Whose Little Girl Are You?   121

On My Way
Up From Eden

CHAPTER ONE

WOMAN AS MOON GODDESS

What Is Femininity, and Who Should Have It?

Genesis 1: 16 (RSV): And God made the two great lights, the greater light to rule the day, and the lesser light to rule the night.

Genesis 5: 1, 2 (RSV): When God created man, he made him in the likeness of God. Male and female he created them, and he blessed them and named them Man when they were created.

CHAPTER ONE

Woman as Moon Goddess

A BEAUTIFUL WOMAN proposed to the crusty old wit George Bernard Shaw half a century ago that they should get together and produce a child, combining her beauty with his brains. Declining, Shaw pointed out. "What if the poor child got my beauty and your brains!" That ended it.

If Shaw had accepted the offer and fathered a son, the brains would have been what counted. Men are valued much more for their intelligence and talent than for their beauty. But if Shaw had fathered a little girl, the beauty would have counted most from babyhood on. A gorgeous girl is a sought-after object anywhere.

IT PAYS TO BE PRETTY

According to Sophie Tucker, a girl's best asset from birth to 18 is good parents. From 18 to 35 she needs good looks. From 35 to 55, she needs a good personality. And from 55 on, she needs good cash.

A realistic Christian today could argue with Miss Tucker that a girl's main need at any age is a good relationship with God, and also that good looks are at least as important as personality after 35. But by and large Miss Tucker was right.

Hard work and good brains and a loving spirit are not the most highly rewarded assets on the marriage market. (Check the list of characteristics that corporations list for ideal corporate executives' wives.) And financial success in the marriage market is generally what keeps fortunate elderly widows safe from the poverty, malnutrition, and neglect that await so many old women today.

"Of course I'd like to be independently wealthy," a pretty graduate student said to me with a twinkle, "but I'd settle for becoming dependently wealthy instead." Studies show that pretty young women are the ones with greatest upward mobility in our society. Especially those who purposely go where wealthy men will meet them. Consider Cinderella. She went to the royal ball. (Plain girls with good personalities and big feet need not apply to the prince.)

Pity George Bernard Shaw's daughter if she had inherited his brains and his face. A smart ugly woman is scary, because devalued people are always subtly threatening to those who look down on them. As a child I often heard Eleanor Roosevelt scorned and criticized.

"Why doesn't that ugly woman stay home and keep quiet?" they exclaimed. "What a face!" Considering myself an ugly child because of my thick glasses, I listened quietly. I stayed quiet for years.

IT COSTS TO BE PRETTY

Of course a smart woman with enough time, money, and determination can de-uglify herself today with scientific help. Skin-deep beauty is one of the big businesses in the United States. So big that Revlon Cosmetics could afford to pay the nation's top model, Lauren Hutton, $200,000 a year for only 30 days of picture-taking to advertise one line of Revlon products. That is almost $4,000 a week all year long for only 30 days of work. (Miss Hutton can blithely spend the rest of her time acting in movies and spending her money.)

The businessmen who run Revlon figure that Miss Hutton's face alone will bring in far above $200,000 in extra profits on their Ultima products. Miss Hutton, a natural beauty (an ex-Playboy bunny), offers every plain woman the dream of becoming a moon goddess. There is a fortune in moisturizers and moon drops.

There's an eternity in it, too. The average American woman reportedly spends two hours daily on grooming—not counting the time spent shopping or sewing. This means one-eighth of her waking hours. If she lives to the age of 70, it means at least seven solid years. Quite a tithe. Needless to say, putting beauty on the face can take time away from pursuits that put beauty into a face.

Once a friend of mine who was getting along in her twenties resorted to an expensive "finishing course." Before that she was one of those sweet, wholesome girls who don't attract much attention. She had spent a year in seminary. In her modeling course she acquired a definite aura of style and sophistication, and it worked. In a year she was married to a Baptist minister. "John Robert Powers" got her into the full-time Christian service she was suited for.

Many of the attractive Christian women in my church spend about ten dollars a week just getting their hair fixed in beauty parlors. One had her perfectly acceptable nose bobbed, and one had her aging facial skin sanded away by a plastic surgeon. (It worked!) Diet pills, contact lenses, wigs, orthodontia, electrolysis, and dermatology come into play. My friends are not yet at the face-lift stage, but as the years go by, I expect a preview of the Rapture; the faces will rise first.

These women are not especially vain, frivolous, or extravagant. They are obeying the eleventh commandment for women: "Be as pretty as you can be." Their husbands are busy obeying the eleventh commandment for men: "Be as successful as you can be." Usually his financial success adds to her purchasable beauty, and her beauty adds to his sense of success.

I wouldn't ever attack success and beauty. I just wonder about them sometimes.

SWEET COMPETITION

One problem with the success and beauty social motif is that as man's personality and status stay the same or very likely improve with age, woman's outward beauty decreases every year beyond maturity. That's why women run so fast to stay in place. That is why, as C. S. Lewis says, a society which tolerates unfaithfulness in marriage (including divorce and remarriage) must always in the long run be unfair to women.

Lewis didn't condemn women for their increasingly crude efforts to be provocative. (I have seen many sad, stiff platinum-blonde women with long black lashes and wrinkled skin, age-spotted hands aglitter with huge rings, tight bright clothes, and a valiant effort to look not-tired.)

"These signs of desperate competition," said Lewis, "fill me with pity." He was not being sarcastic. As an untidy, bulky, balding old bachelor, he was pursued by a few women. Bulky old single women don't get pursued by anyone but purse snatchers.

Being at a disadvantage, women try harder. The old advice was: "Girls, be witty if you must, pretty if you can, but sweet if it kills you!" As advice goes, it is still fairly sage. In fact, some popular new books and courses for women are really little more than detailed elaborations of that one sentence. These books tell women how to please men. Sweetness, whether it is fluttery femininity or a less innocent kind of sexiness, is sometimes worth reading a book or even risking death ("if it kills you") to acquire. And it might mean a small kind of death for those women who are naturally direct, practical, and outspoken.

Woman as Moon Goddess

SEXIST MOONSHINE

"Moonish" is an actual word. Its definitions are capricious, inconstant, and fully round or plump and soft. Which sex is that? There is no such word as "sunnish," but if there were it would probably mean strong, constant, burning, and happy. We are taught from childhood that daughters are moonish and sons are sunnish.

One of the first songs I ever learned went, "Woman is changeable, light as a feather, false as fair weather, who can believe her?" I liked the tune, and so I thought about the words a lot. I sincerely hoped to become light as a feather and false as fair weather, whatever that meant. I didn't know that the song was from an Italian opera and was sung in jest. But similar ideas are all around us, neither in music nor in jest.

In the superb Random House unabridged dictionary, one definition of the verb "to moon" is: "to act or wander abstractedly or listlessly, as in *She was mooning about all day*." Why she? The next definition for the same verb is: "to sentimentalize or remember nostalgically, as in *She spent the day mooning about her lost love*." I immediately wondered if she might just be anemic.

Intrigued, I searched all the rest of page 929 for other ministories about men or women. All I found were four important or genial men: *"He became a monument in his own lifetime." "He certainly was in a mellow mood today." "The President tried to gauge the mood of the country before proposing the bill." "He was in a receptive mood."*

Obviously it is unfair to judge Random House from one random page, and so I tried page 179, also at random. There I found only three vignettes about men and women on the entire page. First, *"She beat her brains out studying, but couldn't keep up with the rest of the class."* (Low thyroid?) *"He refused to prepare for the exam but counted on being able to pick his roommate's brains."* (The clever scoundrel.) And finally, *"He*

17

is thinking of branching out by opening another restaurant in the suburbs." Can this pitiful woman get a job as a waitress in his new restaurant? I wondered. What will become of her? Someone else can survey the other 1,662 pages of the dictionary and seek the answers. It is too threatening to me.

"Moony" is another word that refers to characteristics of the moon. The informal definition is "dreamy, listless, or silly." There is the Ultima ideal woman for you, spoiled and luminous and moony as can be, with empty head and idle hands, while the ideal man is busy proposing bills in Washington, D. C., or branching out in the suburbs. There are few books more interesting than a good dictionary.

VIVE LA DIFFERENCE!

There is a great difference between the sun and the moon, of course, and a great difference between men and women. But they are different differences.

"Men and women are more alike than different!" some feminists declare. That seemed apparent since Genesis 1. It surely is a point to remember. It's more than you can say for the sun and moon relationship.

"Men and women are biologically different!" some antifeminists remind us enthusiastically. I remember the old Thurber cartoon of a woman at a cocktail party confiding to a man, "I love the idea of there being two sexes, don't you?"

It *is* quite an idea, and one not frequently forgotten.

Aside from the clearly visible biological differences, there is the invisible chromosomal difference in every cell in the body. The twenty-fourth pair of chromosomes in a woman is called a pair of X chromosomes. The twenty-fourth pair of chromosomes in a man is an XY pair. So it is that final forty-eighth chromosome that determines the sex of the person. It all depends upon whether the one successful sperm in a million happened to carry an X or a Y within.

Woman as Moon Goddess

How much difference the fatal Y makes, we don't know in full. To begin with, more males than females are stillborn. Next, more males than females are lost to "sudden crib death." Studies show that male babies are more active from their earliest days. From there on it gets harder to distinguish the effects of the Y chromosome from the entire effects of home-conditioning, so far as personality goes. As the quiet mother of two very rowdy boys, I am of the personal opinion that the Y chromosome is a very potent little conditioner of the entire home! It seems that the Y gives males a different androgen/estrogen ratio from females, and that is why males are more aggressive. There is some evidence today that the few unfortunate men who get an extra Y by accident often turn out to be killers.

Some teachers tell us that men and women are inherently different psychologically—profoundly and almost mystically different. Freud said in frustration near the end of his life, "What do women want?" (He had long claimed that they wanted a penis. Did he finally come to doubt it?) His old pupil Carl Jung, who broke with him, came up with some tentative answers about women. Women, he said, have a different kind of basic consciousness from men. Women are the opposite of men in that they have a feminine conscious and a masculine unconscious. (Men have a masculine conscious and a feminine unconscious.)

YIN, YANG, AND JUNG

Traditionally, it is the hero in man that makes him really male. The impulse to overcome danger and difficulties is built into the structure of the masculine psyche. Man is always exploring and changing his environment. Criminals are really failed heroes.

Women, on the other hand, are most concerned with security for their own families. They are often inarticulate about things that really matter most to them. Women have a great capacity to give. Women have a kind of "diffuse awareness" that is the opposite of man's "focused consciousness." That is why a woman who feels a valuable idea pushing its way up in the dark in her deep mind may feel crushed and battered if a man hurls a mass of logic at her at that time.

A woman who excels at math has mastered a masculine skill. A man who is a dancer or artist has developed his feminine gifts along with his masculinity. A woman who gets bossy or talks too much, especially if she quotes inappropriate maxims (or Bible verses?), is not being directed by her true self. A woman who cries is in touch with herself. Women are naturally more gentle, sensitive, and loving than men. These are a few of the Jungian teachings about women.

Why should we as Christians care about Jung's questionable theories of male and female? Because they jibe with some ancient superstitious wisdom and some new scientific findings.

Many old cultures and some modern theorists divide certain characteristics into two sets of opposites:

FEMININE	MASCULINE
dark	light
moon	sun
dream	reason
matter	energy
motherhood	fatherhood
intuition	logic
left hand	right hand
passive	active
images	words
art	science
music (untrained)	mathematics
in space	in time
eternity	history

Woman as Moon Goddess

```
receptive........................... aggressive
diffuse............................. focused
experience ......................... argument
```

In Eastern thought the feminine list is called Yin and the masculine list is called Yang. The well-known symbol for Yin and Yang together making a unity is like a circle with two tadpoles curved within it. I used to think that symbol was a pagan hex of some kind. I realize now that it is more like a philosophical diagram of the two genders of reality. More sex than hex.

BRAINPOWER

The peculiar thing about all this mumbo jumbo is that it coincides very closely with some fascinating new discoveries about the human brain. It has always been known that the brain comes in two matching halves, one on the right and one on the left. The two halves are only joined by one bundle of intricate nerves which carry fantastically complicated messages back and forth instantly from one half to the other. (This connector is called the "corpus callosum.")

We have long known that the right half of the brain largely controls the left half of the body and the left half of the brain largely controls the right half of the body. So a person whose left-brain hemisphere is dominant finds himself right-handed, right-footed, and right-eyed. That fact gives people the false impression that the two brain halves are mirror images of each other and do the same kind of work. That would be neat.

Our newest facts about the brain are weird and alarming. It started in 1864 when a neurologist noted that a woman with a tumor in the right half of her brain lost her ability to recognize people. Since then increasing evidence from brain-damaged people has helped to locate mental abilities. It is found that an injury to the right hemisphere of the brain may cause confusion in spatial awareness, loss of musical ability, lack of recognition, and disturbed awareness of one's own body. That explains why one man who suffered a stroke seemed completely intelligent to his wife while discussing his need for medical care, but was at a total loss when he tried to get dressed to go to the doctor. He was not paralyzed; he couldn't figure out how to change clothes. After a half hour with nothing done, his distraught wife had to take off his pajamas and dress him herself.

In contrast, damage in the left hemisphere can confuse or destroy a person's mathematical or verbal ability. When I married my husband, we received a handwritten note from his proud old grandmother in a Minneapolis rest home. She wrote, "Mr. and Mrs. John S. Lindskoog. I say det ta Johnny and Kay, got for der gabaoga and bags ta grass deg nargdan?"

Rather shaken, I wrote and thanked her for her greeting. She eventually lost her ability to talk or write at all. On her deathbed, her daughter held her hand and said, "Mother, are you trusting Christ now for your salvation? Are you going to be with the Lord?" And the dying woman, who had always claimed that being born a Lutheran was good enough, looked at her daughter through tears and pressed her hand to say yes.

BRAINSTORMING

Incredible as it seems, doctors have dared to cut the cord between the two halves of the brain in a few severe epilepsy patients in hopes that it would relieve their attacks by isolating the storm on one side, allowing the other side to take over and seek medication or other help.

These patients have not only been relieved as hoped, but they seem mentally normal in most ways. Remember that they are walking around with completely split brains! It is said that one of these patients got so angry at his wife once that his passionate right brain was trying to choke her with his left

Woman as Moon Goddess

hand while his logical left brain was trying to protect her with his right hand. But ordinarily this split shows up only in special laboratory tests.

If the patient is given an unseen comb to hold in his right hand, he can describe it in words because he is using the left side of his brain. But if he holds the unseen comb in his left hand he cannot describe it in words because he is feeling it with the right side of his brain, which lacks words. However, if he is shown a group of objects, he can correctly point to a comb to show what he had been feeling in his left hand.

Another simple but chilling result is that after the split a person can still write words with his right hand, but he has lost his ability to draw with it. He cannot even copy a square; that shape in space is incomprehensible to his left brain. With his left hand it is just the opposite; he can copy figures and draw fairly well, but he cannot copy a written word! Split-brain people can understand simple words with their right brain, but they cannot respond from their right brain in words. I think of the old grandmother pressing her daughter's hand to say yes that she was saved.

There are other bizarre and complicated tests for split-brain people. Some actual scenes have been broadcast on educational television as part of a college psychology course.

All of these left-right examples refer to perhaps 95 percent of the population. Just as some people are left-handed, some people have alternative divisions of specialization between their two brain hemispheres. Fortunately, if a child receives an injury on one side of his brain, the other side will frequently develop the ability which would have been lost.

THERE IS NO BETTER HALF

Perhaps the most surprising thing of all about split-brain people is that their left brains seem to hold biologically what the Orientals call Yang and what we call masculine, and their right brains seem to hold biologically what is called Yin or feminine. The left is intellect and the right is "heart." The left is rational, and the right is feeling. The right also seems to be the seat of dreams, because split-brain patients say they are never aware of dreaming again.

It was Albert Einstein himself who said of his own creative processes, "The really valuable thing is intuition"! Intuition is often considered a joke in our culture by people who think of it as a female superstition. Actually, it is a special kind of intelligence that sometimes leaps ahead of ordinary figuring and planning, that sometimes penetrates to hidden truth. It seems to be linked to the right side of the brain.

I heard once that a woman asked Einstein what childhood reading would be most apt to foster scientific ability in young people.

"Fairy tales," he answered. (Fairy tales are notorious stimulants of the illogical subconscious mental forces within us.)

"What else?" she asked, unsatisfied.

"More fairy tales," he replied.

"And then what?" she pleaded.

"More fairy tales!"

RIB LIB

When I was young I was taught by someone at church (far removed from Einstein) that men actually have one rib fewer than women do—proof that the Genesis 2 account is true. I assumed for years that all men had slightly lopsided chests because of Adam's gift to Eve; I felt much obliged. I would have been even more convinced of the truth of Genesis 2 if all women had only one rib, but I could tell that wasn't true. This fable about men's ribs was an innocent and forgivable mistake. After all, Aristotle was one of the wisest men who ever lived, and he thought women had fewer teeth than men.

Woman as Moon Goddess

Once you have a good theory with a rational basis, why bother to count?

I suspect that if a little had been known about human brains in my church when I was young, I might have been taught that the right hemisphere is for women and the left is for men. (In fact, I suspect that there is a useful but dangerous grain of truth in the idea.) Ideal proof would be that most women are left-handed, but there again ideal proof is lacking. No biological difference between the brains in male and female bodies has yet been discovered. Bone structure varies enough that doctors can tell the sex of a skeleton. But dead bones don't give much basis for assigning live mental roles.

The fact that the brains of blacks tend to weigh just slightly less than those of whites would have been useful in the antebellum South, but it is a useless fact to men of good will in our day. If female brains weigh slightly less than male brains, or if they are ever found to have fewer neurons, that may be useful knowledge to male supremacists. Far better for male superiority in our rational culture if all our brains were physically lopsided to the right or left according to our sex. That could even keep women out of college because college is predominantly for left-hemisphere activity. (There people can learn about some of the amazing achievements of people who fully utilize their right hemispheres.)

BISEXUAL BRAINS

But here we are, male and female, with two big healthy hemispheres inside our heads. Each one of us has a "sun brain" and "moon brain" within his inner sky. God made us that way. Both are to be used and valued. As C. S. Lewis remarked, it is the most purely feminine women and the most purely masculine men who are always the most dull. Needless to say, he was not suggesting that interesting men are effeminate and petty or that interesting women are masculinized and callous. He meant that interesting men are sensitive and interesting women are strong.

A century ago the American poet James Russell Lowell wrote about the greater author, Nathaniel Hawthorne:

> When Nature was shaping him, clay was not granted
> For making so full-sized a man as she wanted.
> So, to fill out her model, a little she spared
> From some finer-grained stuff for a woman prepared.
> And she could not have hit a more excellent plan
> For making him fully and perfectly man . . . .
> (from *A Fable for Critics*)

In 1918 H. L. Mencken declared, "Find me an intelligent man, a man free from sentimentality and illusion, a man hard to deceive, a man of first class, and I'll show you a man with a wide streak of woman in him."

And clear back around 1800 Samuel Taylor Coleridge came right out and said that great minds are androgynous! Neuter would have meant sexless, but androgynous means a combination of masculine and feminine. Coleridge, of course, could not know what we know of the physical brain with its masculine side and feminine side. He must have been speaking from observation of his own mind as well as the minds of his brilliant wife and friends. If he could have seen into the future, he would have been speaking of Einstein too.

MATH AND MURDER

There is no doubt that the United States has glorified the functions of the left half of the brain and somewhat devalued the right. British author J. B. Priestley feels that the most urgent need in our civilization is to correct the balance between the masculine and feminine principles.

I can think of two vivid examples of the contrast between the masculine and feminine modes of thinking. One day recently a friend who is a professor entertained me by showing me how to make a Mobius Strip. We took a strip of paper about two inches wide and a foot long, twisted it once, then joined the ends together with tape.

"This paper now has only one side," he said, smiling. "I'll prove it. So long as you can draw a line on the paper without lifting your pencil you are on one side, right?" I didn't answer. Then he drew a line down the center of the paper, on and on, until the line ended where it had begun, and the entire paper was marked with a line two feet long. The Mobius Strip is a mathematical figure famous for its unique single side.

"I don't know any such rule about pencil lines," I responded. "To me the paper has two sides" (I reached out and pinched it), "because I can feel them both between my thumb and forefinger." A typical right-hemisphere response, I realized humbly. We had no argument. The professor and I respect and enjoy each other.

The next example is morbid in more ways than one. In the summer of 1973 a paroled rapist murdered several people in New York State. He was apprehended for only one of the slayings; his lawyers learned from him about the others. Following his directions, they went out and located two young girls' decomposing bodies in different locations and even took pictures.

Both sets of girls' parents, unknown to each other, were desperately seeking their missing daughters. The father of one of them even flew from his home in Illinois to see the rapist's lawyers in New York State to beg for information because he suspected a connection between the known murder and his daughter's disappearance in the same area on a camping trip.

The lawyers refused to tell the parents anything. Nine months later, the murderer himself blurted out the truth on the witness stand.

The bereaved parents were horrified that the lawyers had let them go through nine months of fruitless searching and heartbreak while their daughters' bodies rotted away unburied. The lawyers reasoned that their first duty was to their client. Even an anonymous reporting of the location of the bodies could conceivably have yielded a minute clue to tie their client to the crime and lead to his conviction. Their whole purpose was to try to set the madman free. The chief lawyer said that his feeling for the parents caused him to lose some sleep, but that he was bound to follow the logic of our adversary system of justice.

As a Columbia law professor summed up the matter, "How do you choose between humanitarian considerations and the principle of confidentiality? One wins in the heart and the other in the head."

How do you choose, indeed.

BACK TO THE MOON

There is no doubt about the masculine orientation of American society. It is overwhelmingly rational, verbal, and mathematical. Those characteristics do not preclude insanity. G. K. Chesterton observed once that great reasoners are often maniacal and that maniacs are commonly great reasoners. He wrote a whole chapter in *Orthodoxy* about that subject.

One psychoanalyst had her own theory about why the United States spent a fortune to send men to the moon. It was a secret symbol, she speculated, of Western man's deep need to explore the unpredictable half-light of his own feminine nature. Could the simultaneous craze for astrology spring from the same need?

Incidentally, it is not only women whose physical lives are

tied to the changes of the moon. Statistics show that crimes of violence are much more frequent during a full moon, and they are usually committed by men. (Most murderers are men, and most victims are women.) Furthermore, a psychologist once gave an intelligence test to a mixed class on a night when the moon was dark. When the moon was full he repeated the test. He made sure that every factor was the same except the moon outside, which the students could not see. Every score went up when the moon was full! The practical conclusion is that it is wise to stay off city streets and to do your difficult mental work on nights when the moon is full.

THE FEMININE MISTAKE

Many women find it delightful to be a right-hemisphere moon goddess part of the time in one way or another. I remember the time my husband declared logically after two hours of frustrating work that there was no possible way for our doorbell ever to work again because of a severed wire in the wall. I had a funny hunch that a bit of floral wax would work, and I fixed it in 20 minutes. "It can't hold," he ventured incredulously. That was eight years ago. Moon magic?

I don't run all my life on hunches and dabs of wax. The bright harsh daylight of left-hemisphere rationality is a large part of any sane person's mind. It is how one balances and blends the two modes of consciousness that makes for creativity and skill.

In contrast, confusing or inappropriately mixing the two kinds of intelligence is said to cause trouble. I read once that when a woman asks her husband which is more important to him, she or his work, she is speaking on the feminine level. If he is at all sensitive he will answer her on her level, "You are, of course." But if she then quickly demands that he should therefore put her first and cut down on time and energy for his work, she has unintentionally tricked him by jumping to the everyday level of consciousness where his work possibly needs first place. He will resent this. She may have hurt their relationship instead of helped it.

I never forget the story of a dreamy young wife of a wealthy older man. She loved him very much.

One day he asked her, "Darling, would you still love me if I lost all my money?"

"Yes, of course," she replied with a kiss.

"And would you love me if I became an invalid?"

"I will always love you," she responded.

"And if I were later to become blind and deaf?" he pursued.

"Dear, of course I would love you and care for you."

"And if I finally lost my mind?"

"Don't be ridiculous! Who could love an old, penniless, blind, deaf imbecile!"

So much for the moon goddess. This calls for the earth mother.

CHAPTER TWO

WOMAN AS EARTH MOTHER

What Is a Nurturing Parent, and Who Should Be One?

Proverbs 31: 28, 29 (RSV): Her children rise up and call her blessed; her husband also, and he praises her: "Many women have done excellently, but you surpass them all."

CHAPTER TWO

Woman as Earth Mother

MY NURSE was an earth-mother type if there ever was one.

"Poor thing," she said warmly when they wheeled my hospital roommate away to surgery. "I've seen them come and I've seen them go. In 18 years of nursing, I've seen a lot."

She knew more about my roommate than I did, it turned out, because the young patient was not to return.

"Eighteen years?" I asked. I liked her voice.

"Yes. Three at St. Mary's, seven at St. Joseph's, and eight here."

She shook her head again at my roommate's empty bed and started to bustle out.

"Do you like the nursing profession?" I asked.

"Like it?" she exclaimed. She looked at me strangely, as if the question made no sense. "Honey, anybody can be a nurse if they've been a mother. Being a nurse is just loving people."

STOP ME IF YOU'VE HEARD THIS ONE

That motherly nurse will always remind me of one of my favorite riddles. Unfortunately, the riddle has become so popular that it may soon wear itself out.

A man and his son were in a bad auto accident. The father

was killed, and the son was rushed to a hospital for emergency surgery. In the operating room the surgeon looked at the boy and said, "Call another surgeon. I cannot operate on this boy. He is my son."

How could that be?

The surgeon was the boy's mother, of course.

We have peculiar sex stereotypes in our land. In Russia, where most doctors are women, the riddle wouldn't be worth a thin kopek. Anyone would know the answer right off and would say, "But of course. Is that all?"

Personally, if I ever have surgery, I would rather like to be operated on by a person who can say, "Being a surgeon is just a way of loving people."

LESS THAN A WOMAN

Loving people comes easily to me, but when I was 24 and not yet married, our culture told me loud and clear that a woman is not a real woman until she has slept with a man. There are songs and films about that idea. I have heard a song that claims that a woman is still not a real woman until she has slept with the *right* man. Even in church the required state of virginity was clearly considered a very inferior state. "An unmarried woman is not a whole person." That was pure nonsense, but any nonsense makes you feel inferior if you hear it enough.

I thought marriage would put me on the approved list, but from the wedding shower on I was asked frequently (less frequently but more anxiously as years went by) how soon we would have a baby. A marriage isn't complete until there is a baby in the house, I learned to my dismay. A wife isn't unselfish until she is also a mother. Actually, I felt a very maternal kind of love and concern for the students I taught at school, although most of them were bigger than I was. But you don't tell people that.

Woman as Earth Mother

It happened that for each year I taught, one of my students died. Sterling turned a pickup over. He had failed at everything else; he even failed as a driver. Ernie had appendicitis. His huge dark eyes look at me quietly in my memory. That went on for five years. Then one of my husband's pupils died from spoiled soup on a Scout campout. I remember pouring out my troubled sorrow to my husband then.

"I couldn't tell that those particular lives would be cut short. I tried to serve them, but I was preparing them for life, not for death. Did I fail them?" I still bitterly regretted isolating incorrigible Sterling at the back of the classroom.

"It's those who live the longest who will be influenced most by the kind of nurture you gave them," he answered. "They are the ones who will do the most good for themselves and others, or cause the most hurt to themselves and others. You can't convert people in the classroom; your job is to plant seeds. Teach with living in mind."

I taught well over a thousand teenage children. I cared about every one.

LESS THAN A MOTHER

At last we adopted an adorable baby boy. When he had been with us only 24 hours, my husband said, "Pretend that the agency made a mistake and had to come to get Jonathan today and leave us another baby instead. How would you feel?"

As I recall, my answer was a torrent of tears. This very special individual baby was so much a part of me already that no baby in the world could have taken his place.

I felt strongly that I could successfully nurse him if I tried, but I had always heard that was impossible. I should have trusted my feelings more; I have learned now that for some adoptive mothers with determination breast-feeding is indeed possible. I was as much a mother as one can be, drunk with the wonder of maternal love.

And then a dear relative said coldly, "Well, you'll never know real motherhood if you can't give birth to the baby yourself."

It was one of the first times I ever thought an expletive deleted. It was then I knew for sure that I would never make the grade socially as everybody's real woman. It was small comfort at the time to know that I must have a lot of company.

Even my pediatrician put me down. I got the message that 29 is too old to start mothering very skillfully, especially adoptive mothering. I was assumed to be over-anxious, nervous, and silly. My words were clearly discounted. The fact is that I was never nervous around my baby, but I was soon nervous around my baby's doctor. Eventually the doctor's attitude toward me almost caused my child's death, because my desperate reports of his one serious illness were brushed aside until it was almost too late. That is what stereotyping can lead to.

All this less-than-a-mother business was ironic. Although outwardly I am small and fragile, inside I feel like a great capacious earth mother, with lap and milk enough for all the orphans in the world.

SOME WOMEN DON'T

When Jonathan was six, one day I thundered in frustration, "Why did you pull up all my new little plants?" I had found them lying dead in a row.

"Well, some boys do and some boys don't," he answered philosophically. His answer was really much better than my question, and it applies to many situations. For example, when it comes to mothering active, curious little boys, some women do and some women don't.

Woman as Earth Mother

I remember a married friend who had a healthy nine-year-old son.

"I only got pregnant because so many people urged me to have a baby," she told me frankly. "They said I would be glad if I did and forever sorry if I didn't. A lot they knew about it. Having a baby is the worst thing that ever happened to me. And it can never be undone. I love Brandon so much I would die for him, but I hate having to be his mother. I don't really like children."

Another friend confided once, "I had two abortions when I was younger, and if I had been able to look ahead I would have made it three. My son has turned out fine, but I'm glad he's almost grown. I'm not the mother type."

I have another friend who finds one child nerve-wracking even with a live-in maid to care for him and clean house.

If someone ever says to me, "Woman is at heart a mother," I am going to answer, "Which woman?" Just as women all have vocal chords but some cannot sing well, so all women have reproductive organs but some cannot mother well. We are not all gifted in the same ways. It's no use pretending otherwise.

PRECIOUS IN HIS SIGHT

It seems as if nothing is more treasured or more despised than children. The black market baby racket has been busy selling infants in the United States for up to $25,000 per child. It is obvious that at some inflationary point far below $25,000, "adoption" becomes "child-buying." Tighter laws may clamp down on this kind of high-profit secret baby placement.

No medical treatments are too expensive for the children who come into the right homes. Nothing is too good for them. A rich family in Italy recently paid over three million dollars for the return of their six-year-old boy. No one can accuse them of overvaluing him.

In church we believe the song we teach our children:

> Jesus loves the little children,
> All the children of the world.
> Red and yellow, black and white,
> They are precious in his sight,
> Jesus loves the little children of the world.

Nevertheless, recent studies show that up to 4,000 children a year are killed by their parents in this country. As far as I know, the churches haven't said or done anything about it. About 60,000 children suffer dangerously from home beatings, cruelty, or neglect. Some of them are tortured. We also have at least a million abandoned children on hand.

In New York City alone, at least three children are killed by their parents every week. About 14,000 families are on record for abusing, neglecting, or abandoning their children in New York City every year. And there are only 92 social workers assigned to look after these 14,000 sick families. No wonder that babies have been found dead from starvation with hands so dirty the fingers were stuck together and diaper area so untended that the skin was completely gone. Cases like this are documented in many large cities, not just New York.

Senator Mondale started crusading to get something done by the federal government to help abused children. He discovered that the Department of Health, Education and Welfare has almost 109,000 employees, and not one to work full time on this problem. The Nixon administration opposed Senator Mondale's efforts, insisting that the problem should be handled locally as it has been. You know how well that has worked.

I have to push those children out of my mind. But a pretty little preschool boy was beaten to death a mile from my house last year and buried in a shallow grave in the hills nearby. The young mother and her boyfriend were found and sentenced.

And now whenever I drive my own children past that street I shudder. We go that way to music lessons.

Fullness, kindness, protectiveness, warmth, and generosity are earth-mother traits. They are in no way linked to a fertile womb.

MALE MOTHERING

Earth-mother traits are not even linked to sex. It was Christ who said to another sinful city once, "How often would I have gathered your children together as a hen gathers her brood under her wings . . ." (Mt. 23: 37, RSV).

There is a special kind of virility in men who comfort and nurture the young, hurt, and helpless. Perhaps it is because they are secure in their own masculinity. I met a man once who could calm colicky babies by holding them against a certain part of his broad chest. He said it never failed. And when my own second baby was screaming with colic, he took him into his arms and put him right to sleep. (I wished that I could hire him to stay at our house for three months, but he was a busy engineer.)

Harry Holt was a successful middle-aged Oregon man who loved children so much that he adopted eight Korean orphans and then used all his money and the rest of his life saving as many more as he could. He gathered them into a temporary shelter, later replaced with good buildings, and nursed them back to health (his two daughters were nurses), preparing them to pass the rigid immigration laws for entry into the United States.

"I never turn away a child," he said, and so he made a permanent home in Korea for the retarded who were unadoptable. He hated the red tape that delayed adoptions so long that some adoptable children died of local diseases before they could be sent to waiting families. He slept in a room with 20 cots so that the children who had night fears or minor illnesses would have him right with them all night long.

Altogether Mr. Holt managed to place two to three thousand orphans into Evangelical Christian homes in the United States before he died of a heart attack caused by overwork. (He knew all along that he had a serious heart condition.) His adoption agency is still carrying on the work.

He reminds me of the words of another man, George Matheson:

> Send me, Lord, to the hearts without a home,
> To the lives without a love,
> To the crowd without a compass,
> To the ranks without a refuge,
> Send me to the children whom none have blessed.
> To the famished whom none have fed,
> To the sick whom none have visited,
> To the sinners whom none have claimed,
> To the fallen whom none have lifted,
> To the bereaved whom none have comforted.

TRAVELING THE FARTHEST

I once attended the 15-year reunion of my high school class. After dinner the master of ceremonies, a local policeman, asked routine questions such as which class members had traveled the farthest.

"And which of you has the oldest children?" he asked, then winked broadly and added with a swagger, "Fellows, don't include all the kids we left in Korea. They'll soon be in high school themselves!" Some laughter.

I almost vomited chicken-fried steak and peas all over the white linen tablecloth. These children in Korea and Vietnam eat garbage and wear rags and die by the thousands. We sat stuffed and sumptuous in an expensive hotel, laughing at them.

Woman as Earth Mother

I remember the wistful words of one homeless, illiterate shoeshine boy, "I think of my father's country as a wonderful place, and I wish to go there sometime." This child doesn't even know his own name, but the other boys called him "Mixed Blood" because he is white-skinned. He often goes without supper because he only earns a few cents a day.

The Vietnamese government does next to nothing for orphans. They have almost a million on their hands, not even counting the half-Americans. Their Minister for Veteran Affairs explained once, "Orphans are not producers. They are spenders at a time when we need productive returns on our investments." Fortunately for the government, these nonproducers keep dying.

The United States policy has been that the hundreds of thousands of half-American children are not our concern (not to mention the thousands of Vietnamese children who are left without eyes or hands or feet because of certain kinds of United States bombs). "Our way of doing business," the American Consul General explained once, "is to approach the problem from the point of view of the lawyer and leave social considerations aside."

That is one way of doing business.

Last year my husband kept mentioning one of his high school pupils to me because she gave him special joy. She was not only brilliant, but an unusually dear and beautiful person. One time he also mentioned the fact that she looked Oriental but had an English name.

I remembered a boy with that name whose parents had once adopted four little Korean orphans. My husband inquired. Yes, Sharon was one of the four. She was one of the orphans rescued by Harry Holt.

The reunion I would like to witness someday is the joyful reunion of a few thousand special people with Harry Holt in Heaven. Then there will be real laughter! It will be better than Handel's *Messiah*.

FATHERS WHO WORK

Seven million American families are fatherless. That means seven million American fathers who are somehow deceased or disbursed. One family out of eight is headed by a woman.

A male first-grade teacher in one well-to-do California suburb wrote an article telling what his job is like. To begin with, he plays down his sex in the classroom because he believes it should not make any difference in his profession. But in one way it really does. A third or more of his children do not have a close relationship with any other man. Some of them develop an intense love for him, which creates problems, and some call him "Daddy."

Even in homes which are unbroken, the children often don't get very much fathering. Some fathers with the best of intentions work so hard trying to achieve professional success that they are incapable of giving much of themselves to their children. Anthropologist Margaret Mead asks how a father of four children can possibly compete successfully in his profession. The answer is obvious: by shortchanging the four children. And how many fathers have the best intentions in the first place?

As one family counselor put it in response to the television documentary "An American Family," "We have gone from father as autocrat to father as nothing; we need to find a fatherhood of compassionate but firm discipline and moral fiber." According to this counselor, most sociology experts see the father's abdication from moral responsibility for the raising of children as the source of the great upsurge of young people's troubles today.

Americans today assume that it is traditional for men to have entire responsibility for financial support and for women to have sole responsibility for child nurture. This isn't the way it used to be.

In agricultural communities everyone worked and everyone

cared for the children. I remember seeing an example of this in the cotton fields of Oklahoma when I was a child. Whole families of sharecroppers would be out in the field together all day long doing stoop labor in the hot sun. They were ragged and dusty, and I felt sorry for them. There was usually a baby or a couple of toddlers in a bit of shade at the edge of the field, but the children seven or eight years old were hard at work by their parents. I think now that they were better off than some of the neglected, inept, and pseudo-tough children I see on suburban streets.

There are happier examples than sharecroppers to look at. Prosperous farms and family businesses, for example. Today in America one of the few occupations that offers the chance for both parents to parent equally is college teaching. Some fortunate couples are able to stagger their schedules so that one or the other is always with their small children. The children are twice blessed. Father and mother share both family support and child care. Nice work if you can get it. Perhaps companies will move toward shorter and more flexible work shifts so that more couples can take that option. In Sweden a father can get off work as easily as a mother if there is a sick child to care for!

FATHERS WHO DON'T WORK OUT

Perhaps it is the American father's financial obligation and lack of actual fathering that prompts him to run away. The largest number of people on welfare are families of men who left and don't pay child support. The people who constantly grumble about welfare costs are curiously silent about that fact.

It seems as if many men drift from one wife to another, purposely leaving children scattered along the way to prove something. They prove something, all right. I knew of a man who deserted his wife in an iron lung and left her with six young children to parent alone. Her parenting soon degenerated into screaming in frustration at any child who was within hearing range. Welfare kept them fed and housed and kept the woman alive on her back in the iron lung. The man started a new life elsewhere. The children went wild.

The law allows a man to walk out on his children for no reason and never see them again if that is his pleasure. Who ever heard of a law that would require a father to embrace his children twice every year! All the law asks is that he should contribute to their financial support, and it generally asks that very meekly. Most male judges are very lenient with men who don't make the payments. Destitute mothers don't have the means to fight legally for child support. I have heard a beery construction worker laughing loudly in public about his wife's vain efforts to get child support. In my opinion, if a man can't or won't support his first brood of children, he should be automatically sterilized.

On the other hand, if a man cannot support his children, he should not have to desert them before they can qualify for financial aid. As many observers have stated, the present system actually encourages desertion. It holds a man's right to procreate much higher than the children's right to be fathered.

The Church can stand in vivid contrast to this state of affairs if it wants to. Have you ever seen a team of men running the preschool department? Couples in the nursery? There is a famous young church in our area where many miraculous things have happened. I was told that women do no work at all in the Sunday school there because of Biblical principles of male leadership. That intrigued me. When I looked into it, it was not true at all. All the other wonders were true, but the Sunday school was staffed mainly with women—just like everywhere else.

Children like men. Why not show them in church that men like children and that men like God? First impressions count.

THE SACRED COW

Women are often told by male preachers that nurturing children is woman's highest calling. That saying not only implies that all childless women have missed their real calling, but it also insinuates that men have a different highest calling. I wonder what it is! Perhaps preachers would do better to say that nurturing children is a uniquely sacred task. Period.

One afternoon my four-year-old put on his white terrycloth bathrobe and a pair of rubber boots. He was always inventing costumes. This time he said, "Do I look like God?"

"You always look something like God to me," I said honestly. Few things I say are quite that deeply honest.

"God also wears a crown," Peter reflected, feeling his lack. I looked at his crown of golden curls and kept quiet.

Then he cheerfully explained the costume. "God puts on His rubber boots when He makes a flood."

In C. S. Lewis' famous sermon "The Weight of Glory" he ends by saying that the load or weight or burden of my neighbor's glory should be laid daily on my back, and that only humility can carry it. "There are no *ordinary* people. You have never talked to a mere mortal. . . . Next to the Blessed Sacrament itself, your neighbor is the holiest object presented to your senses."

I assume that for a Protestant, the neighbor is even more holy than the Sacrament. My own feeling is that if my neighbor is a child, especially a child entrusted to me, he is the holiest of all. As Lewis says, every person is on his way toward glory unspeakable or to a nightmare horror, and we are always helping each other toward one destination or the other.

LETTING GO

There is a poem in which Peter Redgrove describes an archaeologist fitting together the ancient bones of a prehistoric woman and tells how he molds a face of wax, overlaying the bones with a semblance of the person who used to be.

> For it is a woman, by the broad hips:
> I give her a smooth skin, and make the mouth mild:
> It is aeons since she saw her child.
> Spinning thin winds of gossamer from his lips.

The poignance underlying every loving motherhood is the fact that it will end.

Once I came to a store counter where a woman was quietly talking with the clerk. "I gave birth to five children, but only two lived past infancy," she concluded. Her teenage daughter standing next to her exclaimed in dismay, "Mother! You never told me there were others!" They left, and I made my purchase deep in thought about the mother and her roundabout public way of revealing her deep losses to her daughter.

Recently a great-great-granddaughter of Queen Victoria gave birth to a baby daughter named Emma. Emma had the use of only a quarter of her brain. She was blind and deaf and could not swallow. She cried pitifully.

Her mother's devotion and intense care kept her alive for nine months, far beyond what the doctors believed possible. At last the mother admitted that her suffering baby could not get better. She gave her barbiturates crushed in milk, wrapped her comfortably, and let her die quickly and painlessly. Then she went on trial for manslaughter. Her friend testified in court, "I have never seen a maternal instinct so strong in any mother." We know it could be true.

The fact that every mother has to let go sooner or later serves as a source of perspective in the following "Mother's Prayer" which was written by someone with limited poetic ability but with very good sense.

Woman as Earth Mother

Give me patience when little hands
Tug at me with ceaseless small demands.
Give me gentle words and smiling eyes
And keep my lips from hasty, sharp replies.
Let me not in weariness, confusion or noise
Obscure my vision from life's fleeting joys
That when in years to come my house is still
Beautiful memories its rooms may fill.

Concentrating on motherhood to the exclusion of other absorbing interests and activities is obviously why many women are left in the lurch after their children grow up. It is a kind of bereavement, especially if there are no grandchildren at hand. As an insurance company ad says, "A child is someone who passes through your life, and then disappears into an adult."

The following dialog is a favorite of mine because it is a goodnatured spoof on overattached mothers. (I cry when I let go of old baby clothes, so count me in.)

MARTHA: No, Charles, not another evening with Joe and Tessie! I'm sick of them.
CHARLES: Come on, honey. We'll have a good time. They are counting on seeing us.
MARTHA: Count me out. I've spent all the time with them that I intend to. We have better friends.
CHARLES: Be a good sport. I know they aren't the best company, but let's do it for old time's sake.
MARTHA: Not the best company? Ha! They are ugly, Charles. They are dull and crude, and you know it. They are low-class, cheap, vulgar bores!
CHARLES: But, Martha! They're our only children . . .

ON MY WAY UP FROM EDEN

TAMMY'S HOPES

A fifth-grade Black girl named Tammy in Atlanta, Georgia, said it all for most women of good will today when she wrote down what her highest hopes are for her future life. She wants to nurture and serve others and to end up as a fulfilled individual who will not be devalued or forgotten.

I hope to be a wife and a mother and I hope to be a good wife and I hope to be a nurse and to help people and want to have a child if it is a her she will be name Angela and if it is a him he will be name Richard and if I finish nurse school and I want to be a nice nurse and help people and then one day I will retire from being a nurse and be a famous person and my name will live forever and forever and the world will think of me as a person.

Good luck, Tammy.

CHAPTER THREE

WOMAN'S FERTILITY RIGHTS

What Does Childbirth Mean Today, And Who Should Reproduce?

Genesis 3: 16 (RSV): To the woman he said, "I will greatly multiply your pain in childbearing; in pain you shall bring forth children. . . ."

Genesis 4: 1, 2 (RSV): She conceived and bore Cain, saying, "I have gotten a man with the help of the Lord." And again, she bore his brother Abel.

Genesis 4: 8 (RSV): And when they were in the field, Cain rose up against his brother Abel, and killed him.

CHAPTER THREE

Woman's Fertility Rights

GOOD NEWS! We humans have fulfilled God's first commandment to us in the Bible. In fact, we seem to have fulfilled it beyond God's wildest imagination. It is true that we have more or less failed to keep all the rest of His commandments, but we keep on keeping His very first one until it is ridiculous. We can stop now.

FILLING THE EARTH

"Be fruitful and multiply and fill the waters in the seas," God said to the sea creatures (Gen. 1: 22, RSV). And they did a beautiful job of it by not taking Him literally. He surely didn't mean for the ocean to be packed like a can of sardines. He meant for it to be teeming with the rich and wonderful system of sea life which we had before we began dumping in DDT, mercury, lead, oil, and excess sewage.

"Be fruitful and multiply, and fill the earth" (Gen. 1: 28, RSV), God told Adam and Eve and their offspring. They multiplied, indeed, and the earth was completely filled by 1850, if we accept the reasonable estimate that God's earth, at least in its fallen state, is only big enough to support one billion people.

No wonder the current situation is called a population explosion. When Christ was born we numbered about a quarter of a billion. Finally in 1650 we had doubled to a half billion. Two hundred years later, in 1850, we had doubled again and hit that ideal one billion. Eighty years later, in 1930, we hit two billion! Now we are at 3.9 billion.

As a result, three-quarters of us will go to bed hungry tonight. Ten thousand people, mostly children, died of starvation today; 10,000 more will starve to death tomorrow and every day. Nevertheless, unless incredible catastrophes or the Second Coming (pray for it) intervene, we will number seven billion in the year 2000. It's a matter of simple mathematics. (No wonder so many people dislike simple mathematics.)

The ordinary person has never seen a million people or a billion people, and so to him the figures may be interchangeable. We hear of so many billions of dollars for defense every year that the immensity of the figure is lost on us. It would help if we all actually counted by ones to a billion. If the proud parents of the world's four-billionth person, soon to be born, were to celebrate the new arrival by giving one penny for food to each underfed person on earth, the gesture would cost the family 30 million dollars. That could mean one morsel of rice or a few drops of milk for every starving person.

MAKE THE WORLD SAFE FOR DEMOGRAPHY

When I once explained to my three-year-old son a bit of the simple physical difference between boys and girls, he clapped his hand to his forehead and exclaimed, "I can't believe it! Mom; you're kidding me." It didn't fit into his view of life.

When my husband once gave a lesson on the population problem to a large adult Sunday school class made up of very intelligent and affluent people, they couldn't believe him and were greatly offended. His facts didn't fit their view of life.

Demography is the science of vital statistics, such as population. Today demographers are the bearers of bad tidings. And you know what happens to the bearers of bad tidings. I recently saw a bumper sticker that said: "May all you damn ecology freaks freeze to death in the dark!" (I reread it three times to make sure.)

For Christians there is an extra threat from the demographers: the fact that the Bible didn't even warn us about overpopulation! Why would God bother to tell us about earthquakes and famines and wars, which were obvious dangers, but fail to mention this ultimate bombshell? If it were true, He would have told us so. After all, we like to think that we have all the inside information about the Last Days. All we can do now is to point out that Malthus was a Christian minister, but we didn't believe him.

All God ever told us in the Bible about reproduction was affirmative indeed. We were all led to desire "arrows in our quivers." Somehow we got the idea that biological procreation was a high duty as well as a privilege. In fact, the poor little church I grew up in always awarded orchids on Mother's Day to mothers of large broods, no matter how inept their mothering was. Some especially fertile women only came on Mother's Day, and a certain amount of rancor developed among the regular worshipers who lost their orchids that way. Anyway, we girls all got the message.

We don't like to be told all of a sudden that motherhood and apple pie have become hazardous to our health because of clogged environment and clogged arteries. That causes future shock.

PRO-CREATION

The simplest way for a Christian to handle the population problem is to embrace a wild faith that God can supply the needs of all mankind no matter how many billions crowd the earth at once. This is the belief of Mother Teresa, a Roman Catholic nun who has given her life to serving the most pitiful people in Calcutta, one of the world's greatest centers of pain, misery, and overpopulation.

"Our way is to preserve life, the life of Christ in every child," she said. Does she think there are too many children in India?

"I do not agree, because God always provides. He provides for the flowers and the birds, for everything in the world that He has created. And those little children are His life. There can never be enough."

It is not easy to scoff at Mother Teresa's simpleminded saintliness. She lives with the poorest of the poor and ministers with joy to the destitute, sick and dying who are found lying in the streets. Her first patient was half eaten by rats and ants. She says, "To children, to the poor, to all who suffer and are lonely, give always a happy smile. Give them not only your care, but also your heart." Perhaps Mother Teresa has a holy wisdom unknown to most demographers and ordinary Christians.

THE MORE THE MERRIER?

In contrast, cat lovers in the United States are upset because over half the cats in our country are homeless. They feel it is wrong for cats to starve and suffer, and for unwanted kittens to perish. Therefore they are setting up clinics where cats can be neutered at low cost in order to cut down the cat population and thus to cut down suffering. We took our cats to the clinic. Our neighbors, who are Roman Catholics, are blessed with a new litter of unwanted kittens every year. Most of the kittens are eventually exterminated. Perhaps they go to heaven.

I am such a softie that I couldn't take a litter of kittens to be killed. I don't even like to thin out a bunch of seedlings.

Woman's Fertility Rights

Every plant lover knows that one or two seeds in a pot can yield good plants, but 1,000 seeds in a pot will yield a sorry crop. This is an example of the law of diminishing returns caused by the limited nature of the resources in the pot—the nutrients and space. Perhaps that law is a result of the fall of man. If it weren't for that law we could feed all the people on earth from one flowerpot! But working with our present limitations, every time we double the population of the world, the world needs twice as many meals, hospitals, schools, jails, homes, beds, boats, clothes, bicycles, toothbrushes, cows, vitamins, churches, and waste-disposal systems. Not to mention insane asylums.

WASTE NOT, WANT NOT

Mother Teresa has a simple Christian answer to the problem. No matter what happens, God will provide for everyone. And anyone who believes that man is only a highly evolved animal has an equally simple solution, if he is not too sentimental. It is one that Jonathan Swift offered in satire in 1729 when there was hunger in Ireland: turn the little children from economic liabilities into economic assets. Sell them to rich Englishmen as a tender table delicacy.

Let childbearing and selling serve the poor as a cottage industry. There could be a compulsory child-harvesting and processing industry in every poor country. A natural corollary would be the recycling of tough-meated elderly people in cans of inexpensive but nutritious stew. At the point of reduced productivity, the aged would thus pass from "eat" to "be eaten" status.

With millions or billions of poor children and old people productively eliminated every year, there will be more air, space, food, and water for the rest of the population. Before long, world population will be stabilized at a billion or so, the haves always eating up all the extra have-nots. That is what they have been doing anyway, figuratively, but this way will be mercifully quicker and less wasteful. B. F. Skinner, author of the book *Beyond Freedom and Dignity*, should enthusiastically approve of this plan—that is, if I understand his book correctly.

ZPG IS NOT A FANCY SPORTS CAR

There is a small group of vocal people located midway between saintly serenity and cannibalism. They are rather drab, practical, conservative people who belong to the Zero Population Growth movement. They urge that we stop our population at four billion rather than trying for eight. They would like to keep famines, wars, and destruction of the earth to a "minimum" this way.

The trouble is that they are asking couples to limit themselves to two offspring, and many people consider them crazy for proposing such a radical idea. An especially popular family plan with couples all over the world is "an heir and a spare." They want two sons, just in case. To get them, couples will on the average produce two sons and two daughters. And that is how we double. Of course, if from this moment on no couple produced more than two children, world population would still increase for 50 to 60 years, because the average person in the world is so young today. (Latin America is almost half children now.) Most young people are going to reproduce now and die later. We will have more births than deaths for a long time. ZPG wants to equalize the births and deaths.

Many people feel that ZPG is audacious to ask them to give up their most basic right to life—the right to reproduce to their heart's content. They are obviously less concerned about every person's right to pure water, clean air, and plenty of wholesome food—or else they haven't yet realized the connection.

A STORY NOT FOR CHILDREN

"Who will stop multiplying and help me to hold down world population at its present level?" asked the little red hen.

"Not I," said the housewife. "Bearing children is my most creative and loving act. It is the meaning of my life."

"Not I," said the self-centered man. "I don't care about the rest of the world. I'll do as I please."

"Not I," said the poor farmer. "I need all the sons I can get to help me grow food and to support me in my old age."

"Not I," said the rich man. "My children all get good nutrition and higher education. They are the cream of the crop."

"Not I," said the third world. "My strength is in numbers; that is the only power or wealth I have. I won't give it up."

"Not I," said the libertine. "I have a sex drive which I need to fulfill. If children are born, it's their problem."

"Not I," said the American Christian. "For a variety of reasons."

"What are they?" asked the little red hen.

"Let me think," said the Christian.

WHAT THE WORLD NEEDS NOW

"The most important reason," Christian began, "is stated in a cute card congratulating new parents. It says, 'A baby! How wonderful! What the world needs is more people like you.' No matter how much of the world's resources our many children use, they will be a unique blessing to the suffering world because of the loving service they will perform. Our best way of helping this overcrowded world is to produce virtuous, godly citizens to influence the next generation."

The little red hen said, "Can't you take in children and orphans and nurture them to become good citizens?"

"That's not the same," Christian answered. "They would not be the offspring of true Christians and could not measure up. God does a supernatural work when children are conceived in Christian marriage. And the genes are better too. The natural parents of the orphans may have taken drugs and damaged the children's chromosomes. These children may have bad blood. They may have social problems because of mixed race. They may have physical problems because of poor nutrition or abuse. They might become a cross for us to bear. Let the non-Christians adopt them.

"Besides," he went on, "a Christian's body is the temple of God. It is a fact that a woman who bears a child has a slightly better chance of avoiding cancer than a barren woman. Therefore Christian women should bear children."

"Wouldn't one be enough?" asked the red hen. "Then you could adopt or take foster children. There are so few Christian foster homes."

WHEN MULTIPLYING MEANS SUBTRACTING

"Well, frankly, many of our Christian families end up a little bigger than we intended even without taking in outsiders. It is often because God fails to give us a child of the sex we hoped for, so we keep trying. But more often it is because the contraceptives failed us once or twice."

"I didn't think a carefully done vasectomy could fail," the hen answered.

"Vasectomy? Well, there's no reason to go that far." Christian frowned. "It costs a man something to get a vasectomy. No, when our imperfect contraceptive methods fail, we take it as God's will. There are a few of us who use none at all, in fact, and just leave the results up to God!"

"Do they go without antifreeze in the winter and hope that God will keep their radiators from freezing?" the hen asked.

"Don't compare the care of a car to the care of the human

body," Christian answered. "The human body is irreplaceable and holy. However, you can't blame people for depending upon special miracles or dumb luck part of the time. It's only natural.

"Besides," Christian went on, "it would do no good at all for some of us to cut down our childbearing in order to take in needy children. The world is awash with needy children. The problem is too big. Our individual sacrifices wouldn't count at all. They are as useless as voting."

"Wouldn't it count to those adopted children or to God?" the hen wondered.

"Besides," Christian went on without answering, "each new baby of ours is so tiny and takes so little from the earth."

"If an American baby lives 70 years," the hen clucked, "he will use directly or indirectly 26 million gallons of water, 21,000 gallons of gasoline, 10,000 pounds of meat, 28,000 pounds of milk and cream, and perhaps $20,000 worth of clothing and furniture, not to mention all the rest. One American Christian uses up the earth's resources and pollutes the air and water more than a dozen pagans in India or Java."

"I wish the pagans would all become impotent!" Christian exclaimed, not at all unkindly. "But surely God wants Christians to multiply. Why, even Shakespeare said, 'Lady, thou art the cruellest she alive, who'd take these beauties to the grave and leave the world no copy.'"

"If every Christian had only two children, that would be two copies," the little hen squawked. "Of course when Shakespeare wrote sonnets to a friend begging her to have offspring, world population was under one-half billion, not four billion. But he also wrote, 'You take my life when you do take the means whereby I live.' Today Americans are taking vastly more than their share of the earth's resources, the means whereby we all live."

The hen ruffled her wings. "Forget Shakespeare. Let me quote you some Bible verses."

ON MY WAY UP FROM EDEN

ZPG BIBLE VERSES

"If any man would come after me, let him deny himself and take up his cross and follow me" (Mt. 16: 24, RSV).

"Whoever receives one such child in my name receives me; but whoever causes one of these little ones who believe in me to sin, it would be better for him to have a great millstone fastened round his neck and to be drowned in the depth of the sea" (Mt. 18: 5, 6, RSV).

"See that you do not despise one of these little ones; for I tell you that in heaven their angels always behold the face of my Father who is in heaven" (Mt. 18: 10, RSV).

"So it is not the will of my Father who is in heaven that one of these little ones should perish" (Mt. 18: 14, RSV).

"Then the righteous will answer him, 'Lord, when did we see thee hungry and feed thee, or thirsty and give thee drink? And when did we see thee a stranger and welcome thee, or naked and clothe thee? And when did we see thee sick or in prison and visit thee?' And the King will answer them, 'Truly, I say to you, as you did it to one of the least of these my brethren, you did it to me' " (Mt. 25: 37-40, RSV).

"For all that is in the world, the lust of the flesh and the lust of the eyes and the pride of life, is not of the Father but is of the world. And the world passes away, and the lust of it; but he who does the will of God abides for ever" (I John 2: 16, 17, RSV).

"By this we know love, that he laid down his life for us; and we ought to lay down our lives for the brethren. But if any one has the world's goods and sees his brother

Woman's Fertility Rights

in need, yet closes his heart against him, how does God's love abide in him? Little children, let us not love in word or speech but in deed and truth" (I John 3: 16-18, RSV).

"Beloved, I beseech you as aliens and exiles to abstain from the passions of the flesh that wage war against your soul. Maintain good conduct among the Gentiles, so that in case they speak against you as wrongdoers, they may see your good deeds and glorify God on the day of visitation" (I Peter 2: 11, 12, RSV).

"The sins of some men are conspicuous, pointing to judgment, but the sins of others appear later. So also good deeds are conspicuous; and even when they are not, they cannot remain hidden" (I Timothy 5: 24, 25, RSV).

"Do not neglect to do good and to share what you have, for such sacrifices are pleasing to God" (Hebrews 13: 16, RSV).

" 'All things are lawful,' but not all things are helpful. 'All things are lawful,' but not all things build up. Let no one seek his own good, but the good of his neighbor" (I Corinthians 10: 23, 24, RSV).

JUMPING TO CONCLUSIONS

"You may be right," said Christian. "I will think about it very hard for a long time."
"There is no more time," said the little red hen.
In a few years the world was suffering widespread famines, revolutions, and breakdown of the ecosystem. The hen returned to her unhappy friends. They were very scared.
"Who will share in a return to open space, clean air, pure water, adequate food, and replenished natural resources?" asked the hen.

"I will," said the housewife.
"I will," said the self-centered man.
"I will," said the poor farmer.
"I will," said the rich man.
"I will," said the third world.
"I will," said the libertine.
"I will," said the American Christian.
"No you won't," said the little red hen. "It's too late."
And it was.
(The moral of this story is: TRY TO DO WHAT IS RIGHT. That's the moral of all good stories, isn't it?)

CHAPTER FOUR

WOMAN'S OBJECTION TO SUBJECTION

How Do Paul's Teachings Relate to Women Today?

II Peter 3: 11-18 (RSV): Since all these things are thus to be dissolved, what sort of persons ought you to be in lives of holiness and godliness, waiting for and hastening the coming of the day of God, because of which the heavens will be kindled and dissolved, and the elements will melt with fire! But according to his promise we wait for new heavens and a new earth in which righteousness dwells.

Therefore, beloved, since you wait for these, be zealous to be found by him without spot or blemish, and at peace. And count the forbearance of our Lord as salvation. So also our beloved brother Paul wrote to you according to the wisdom given him, speaking of this as he does in all his letters. There are some things in them hard to understand, which the ignorant and unstable twist to their own destruction, as they do the other scriptures. You, therefore, beloved, knowing this beforehand, beware lest you be carried away with the error of lawless men and lose your own stability. But grow in the grace and knowledge of our Lord and Savior Jesus Christ.

CHAPTER FOUR

Woman's Objection to Subjection

SOMETIMES PAUL'S WRITTEN TEACHING on women seems like a good news/bad news joke. The good news is: "In Christ Jesus you are all sons of God, through faith. For as many of you as were baptized into Christ have put on Christ. There is neither Jew nor Greek, there is neither slave nor free, there is neither male nor female; for you are all one in Christ Jesus" (Gal. 3: 26-28, RSV). That is the best news in the world for anyone.

PAULINE IS NOT A LADY

The bad news, which Paul added later, is: "Let a woman learn in silence with all submissiveness. I permit no woman to teach or to have authority over men; she is to keep silent. For Adam was formed first, then Eve. If there is anything they desire to know, let them ask their husbands at home. For it is shameful for a woman to speak in church. If a woman will not veil herself, then she should cut off her hair. Let wives also be subject in everything to their husbands" (I Tim. 2: 12, 13; I Cor. 14: 35; 11: 6; Eph. 5: 24, RSV).

The crowning blow—from the man who once claimed: "By grace you have been saved through faith; and this is not your own doing, it is the gift of God—not because of works, lest any man should boast" (Eph. 2: 8, 9, RSV)—is the puzzling passage: "Yet woman will be saved through bearing children, if she continues in faith and love and holiness, with modesty" (I Tim. 2: 15, RSV). Sounds like bad news indeed. How would Christian men like their salvation to hang upon fatherhood (Paul himself was single) and consistent holy living?

Unfortunately, some Evangelical Christians use these Pauline passages about women primarily to prove that it is God's will for Christian women to be permanently subordinate and subservient—if not uneducated—in church, home, and society. Paul's words can be misused against women's rights. They can be misused to show that women should all be enthusiastic cooks, baby-sitters, and home nurses, and they should never excel over men professionally.

As a result, some impatient people misuse the same passages to show that Paul was a cranky old woman-hater whose ideas are all best forgotten. They want to throw the baby out with the bath water. Let's look at some of the bath water.

PROPER CHURCH BEHAVIOR

First and hardest is Paul's advice to Timothy (I Tim. 2: 8-15) about the role of women in church. Paul begins by saying that he wants men to lift their hands up reverently in prayer, with no anger or argument. In the two Bible-believing churches I have belonged to, the part about no anger or argument was taken as an ideal, not a total possibility, and the part about lifted hands was considered a figure of speech or a cultural difference. Our men kept their hands *down* reverently.

Next, Paul recommends that Christian women dress modestly and sensibly, specifically with no braids, no gold, no pearls, and no expensive clothes. (Is a $20 dress expensive today? $50? $100?) The style and attractiveness of these women should be seen in their good deeds, not in their physical appearance. In both Bible-believing churches I have belonged to, the ladies wore fancy hair, gold rings and watches, and stylish clothes (which usually means neither modest nor sensible). And the Christian men wanted it that way.

When I asked about this passage once, I was told it only meant that a female shouldn't spend so much time and money on attire that she couldn't give much time and money to God's work. *If that is what Paul meant, why didn't he say that?* I wondered. According to William Barclay, Paul's rules here exactly fit the culture of the time; he didn't want female Christians to go about looking like extravagant Greek or Roman fashion plates.

One can't help wondering how Paul would feel today about Christian men wearing $8.00 neckties to church and getting there in new $8,000 cars, in terms of ostentatious luxury and popular sex symbols. Who knows.

SILENCE, JUST SO IT'S NOT GOLDEN

Barclay goes on to explain that for a decent Greek woman to take an active part in a meeting would soon have branded her as a loose woman. The early church did not need that kind of reputation. Furthermore, Jewish women, who were classed with children and slaves, had never been allowed to be seen or heard at the synagogue. Since they were not used to taking part in religious instruction, it is understandable that Paul warned them to be silent and respectful.

Accordingly, Paul ruled that women were not to give religious instruction to anyone or to exercise any authority over men. People who quote Paul here in opposition to women elders, administrators, or pastors, must also face up to the question of women Sunday school teachers, conference speakers, missionaries, writers, editors, choir leaders, soloists, and seminary professors—as well as women voters in congregational elections. How would Paul react to Corrie ten Boom's ministry in our day? (I think he would love her.)

I first came across Dr. Samuel Johnson's famous observation about women preachers when I was young, and I used to believe it. He said, "Sir, a woman preaching is like a dog's walking on his hind legs. It is not done well; but you are surprised to find it done at all."

The brilliant Dr. Johnson had a sad and difficult life. For example, he married a woman 20 years his senior. So his crotchetiness is rather understandable. But it seems ironic to hear such a condemnation of women preachers from a man who grew up in the country where Susannah Wesley was preaching from time to time.

Susannah Wesley is known now as the supreme example of good Christian motherhood, and she was also noted then for her fine preaching. This is amazing in that she had 19 children and made it a point to spend an hour alone with each child every week. History tells us how those hours paid off. (Her sons John and Charles were used by God to save thousands of souls.) Yet when Susannah Wesley occasionally filled in as a pulpit substitute for her husband, the congregation came much more eagerly to church. Supposedly she did all this without household help.

I would be relieved to learn that her house was always dusty. All I know is that once it burned flat to the ground, and she took that in stride too. She shows me what Mark Twain meant when he said that few things are harder to put up with than the annoyance of a good example.

UP FROM EDEN

Some Christians can't buy Paul's apparent reasoning in I Timothy 2: 12-14 that women (Corrie ten Boom and Susannah Wesley included) should not speak simply because Eve was created after Adam. Would Paul also argue that Adam should not speak because he was created after the beasts? (If anything, the Genesis pattern of ascending order in creation would indicate Eve's superiority to Adam.) The passage gets even harder. Paul is sounding more like the rabbi Saul and other rabbis of his day than the Paul we know and love. He seems to blame the fall of mankind entirely upon Eve! There and in the following sentence, which seems to make the salvation of women dependent upon both procreation and good works, Bible students offer various views to make sense out of what would seem simple wrong-headedness.

Whether we take I Timothy 2: 15 as an allusion to the Savior of the world being born to Mary or as a defense of marriage or as some other understandable doctrine, we must admit that Paul is not his clearest in this passage, to say the least. Kenneth Taylor tried to make good theology out of it in *The Living Bible* by paraphrasing it as: "So God sent pain and suffering to women when their children are born, but he will save their souls if they trust in him, living quiet, good, and loving lives." It seems an improvement on Paul, but what in the world does Mr. Taylor mean by quiet lives?

EVERYONE TAKE PART (EXCEPT 51 PERCENT)

So much for Paul's advice to Timothy about women. His rules in I Corinthians 14: 26-40 about propriety in Corinthian church meetings includes similar advice. "At all your meetings," Paul began, "let everyone be ready with a psalm or a sermon or a revelation, or ready to use his gift of tongues or to give an interpretation; but it must always be for the common good . . . " (Jerusalem Bible).

In the Bible-believing churches I have belonged to, we never followed this advice, but we always quoted the conclusion, that "God is not a God of confusion," and "all things should be done decently and in order." Throughout this passage Paul is talking about the encouragement and regulation of spiritual gifts at church meetings. He concludes that we should not forbid speaking in tongues in our gatherings. My churches concluded that we *should* forbid it. I asked about that, and I was told that some of Paul's teaching only applied to his own day.

Right in the middle of this brief passage about congregational participation, which Paul claims is a command from the Lord, he agrees with Jewish law that women must keep quiet. If they have any questions, they must ask them to their own husbands at home. This is not only threatening to millions of single women today, but it is no doubt threatening to millions of husbands who are not Bible scholars or profound thinkers. Surely an educated wife must not embarrass her good husband by running circles around him with theological questions. Paul must have been speaking here only to uneducated married women who were unnecessarily interrupting the church meeting.

At the time Paul was writing, Christians still observed the Sabbath in Jewish synagogues, too. Paul never excused them from it. Perhaps Saturday worship and observance of old Jewish rules about women's silence are in the same category, and both were meant to drop away as time passed. I can appreciate people who respond here, "Don't rationalize away the facts! Keep to the Scripture. Don't confuse it with history or conjectures." The trouble is, as C. S. Lewis says, real things are never simple. They may seem simple, but they are not. And of all writers, Paul does not seem simple.

Paul's main point seems to be that it would be shameful or unseemly for women to speak up at meetings. True, it would have been shameful then, when women were uneducated second-class people. The question for us is: "What is shameful and unseemly now?" My three-year-old son was looking at a photo of the inside of our church sanctuary once, and he suddenly asked me with concern, "Mom, why don't they let ladies talk into the microphone there?" I know he loves microphones, and I think he loves ladies.

HATS OFF

We do have a few women speak into the microphone at our church once in awhile. Women have always sung in our church and in almost every church.

But where our church most obviously disobeys Paul is in regard to his very plain words in I Corinthians 11: 2-16. No man is to pray or prophesy with a head-covering on, and no woman is to pray or prophesy without her veil on. (Strange, it sounds here as if she can pray or prophesy aloud when she has her veil on! That is how Bible scholars read it.)

"A woman ought to have a veil on her head, because of the angels" (vs. 10, RSV), Paul explains. It is explanations like this that cause people to tear their hair. I don't know if Paul allowed women to tear their hair or not. He goes on to say that long hair is given to woman for a covering. But if she doesn't cover this proper covering with a veil, according to Paul, she should shave her head and go to church bald; it is that disgraceful for a woman to show her hair in church.

Men, on the other hand, are not to have long hair, and they are not to cover their hair either. It is meant to be short, and it is meant to show. This symbolized to Paul that man is in the image and glory of God. I don't think that Paul thought of God as a man with short hair, and so the symbolism is lost on me. I'm sure the symbolism was meaningful in Paul's day, like the symbolic covering over a woman's hair.

We are ready to agree with Paul's principle rather than his example. It is clear that any socially oppressed group which finds liberation in Christ should not become heady with self-assertion, should avoid the appearance of evil, and should practice restraint and control in order to avoid becoming an offense to the standards of propriety in that culture.

In verse 13 (RSV) Paul asks rhetorically, "Judge for yourselves; is it proper for a woman to pray to God with her head uncovered?"

We did judge for ourselves, Paul. Yes, it's proper.

CROWNS ON

Finally, in his letter to the Ephesians, Paul talks about something basically even more important to most women than their role in church—their role in marriage. And in Ephesians 5, often thought of wryly as bad news for women, we have the really good news about family relationships. How often this chapter is misread with the idea that women are to obey in marriage, which is hard work, and in return men are only to love women as they love their own bodies—which today carries the idea of ownership, neglect, and passing emotions. This makes a parody of what Paul is really saying.

Paul begins here by saying, "Give way *to one another*" (Jerusalem Bible) or "Be subject to *one another* out of reverence for Christ." That command prefaces the next sentence: "Wives, be subject to your husbands, as to the Lord" (Eph. 5: 21, 22, RSV). In a day when a wife had no legal rights in marriage and was hardly more than a piece of property passed from father to husband, Paul sets up submission as a two-way street! This alone ranks him tops as a prophetic marriage counselor in my view. Then he spends about 60 words elaborating a wife's duty to respect her husband and about 110 words elaborating a husband's duty to love his wife. The husband gets the harder assignment.

Paul did not tell the wife to be lovable and the husband to compel respect; he started at the other end! This respect and love does not have to be earned. Giving it freely is inherent in the role of being a Christian wife or husband. Obviously Paul is talking about respect and love that are acts of will, not mere surges of emotion.

During his own brief marriage C. S. Lewis wrote the book *The Four Loves*, and in it he briefly discussed what Paul meant by man's headship in marriage. Nature crowns man with dominance in the act of love, Lewis observed, and Christian law crowns him with headship in marriage. This means that he is to love his wife as Christ loved the Church *and gave His life for her.* This headship of a husband is seen most clearly, he said, in the sorrows of marriage—in a husband's unwearying care for a good wife who is sick and suffering, or his inexhaustible forgiveness for a bad wife. And the husband whose headship is Christlike (the only kind of headship granted) never despairs. C. S. Lewis was writing from real life; his own wife suffered and died from cancer, and he cared for her unwearyingly.

PAUL AND REAL WOMEN

I always like to know how a great teacher treats the people in his own life. Rousseau, for example, wrote and taught marvelous ideas about nature and the needs of people and society and how to rear children. He was a genius. But when his own children were born, he popped them into a foundlings' home and that was the end of them. He didn't have time or money for them, or human compassion either, apparently. He fought terribly with his friends because he had a persecution complex that wouldn't quit. After he was dead, people gradually realized that he had been mad.

Paul was just the opposite. He was obsessed with ideas, like Rousseau, but when he had his "madman's" experience on the road to Damascus, and he saw the risen Christ and was struck blind, he became radiantly sane. When Paul said he was persecuted, he really was!

Although Paul's background as a strict rabbi had taught him to avoid women as his inferiors, he eventually found himself working happily with women in the church. Romans 16 alone shows how highly he esteemed them. When he wrote his letter to the Romans he dictated it to a man named Tertius and then sent it off with a woman named Phebe. In Romans 16 he praised Phebe as one of his helpers. But since Tertius obviously had no carbon paper, what higher praise could Paul bestow upon Phebe than trusting her for weeks on land and sea with the only copy of his most important writing! Some would say it is now the most important book in the Bible.

In the letter itself Paul sent greetings to Mary, a hard worker, and to Tryphaena and Tryphosa and Persis, other female workers in the Lord. He described Junias as an apostle. He also greeted Julia and the mother of Rufus and the sister of Nereus.

And, most surprising, he headed his whole list of bouquets with Priscilla and Aquila—in that order! "Greet Prisca and Aquila, my fellow workers in Christ Jesus, who risked their necks for my life, to whom not only I but also all the churches of the Gentiles give thanks; greet also the church in their house" (RSV).

Priscilla and Aquila were Paul's special friends. When Paul first met them in Acts 18: 2, Aquila was named first. The couple worked together as tentmakers. But only 16 verses later when the three sailed away together on a ship, Priscilla's name already had top billing. She must have been a real woman! She has even been suspected of writing Hebrews. The sober truth is that the teacher Apollos is a more likely candidate for the honor of that accomplishment. It happens that when Apollos was a new Christian, "He began to speak boldly in the synagogue; but when Priscilla and Aquila heard him, they took him and expounded to him the way of God more accurately." So you can't get away from Priscilla's leadership.

But we can try to put her in her place today, since Paul himself didn't see fit to do so. If you look her up in Cruden's concordance, you will find "Priscilla: see Aquila." And under Aquila, the Scripture listings are altered so that his name always comes before hers. I don't think either Priscilla or Aquila would give a tent peg for the honor. When you are busy risking your neck for Paul on earth or busy celebrating the victory with Paul in heaven, such passing distinctions don't matter.

CHRIST AND REAL WOMEN

Why the emphasis upon Paul's attitude toward women, since Christ is the center of Paul's faith and ours? Because Paul left us written teachings about women, and Christ didn't. Christ's only writing that we know of was done when a man and woman were caught in adultery and the woman alone was brought to Him for a verdict. He wrote His comment in the dust.

But we know what He said aloud. His verdict to her accusers was: "He that is without sin among you, let him first cast a stone at her." Since He was the only man present who was without sin, He was soon left alone with the woman. He said, "Go, and sin no more." One is left with a strong conviction that she did just that.

When Jesus talked with the sinful Samaritan woman at the well, His disciples were more shocked because she was a woman than because she was a Samaritan or a sinner. That shows what strong prejudice against women Jesus quietly disregarded in His culture.

When Jesus was visiting His friends Martha and Mary at Bethany once, Martha knocked herself out doing the expected work of an expert housewife and hostess. Meanwhile Mary was attending seminary at the feet of Jesus. When Martha finally complained, Jesus answered, "Mary has chosen the good portion. . . ." Where did He get the idea that Mary had the right to make such a choice? Not from His culture! Perhaps not from ours.

Once a woman in the crowd called out to Him, "Blessed is

the womb that bore you, and the breasts that you sucked!" (Luke 11: 27, RSV). I used to be taught that Jesus then rebuked her because she had spoken loudly and out of turn, but I can't find that in the passage now. All I find is His gentle dismissal of her traditional sex-organ view of woman with the amazing words, "Blessed rather are those who hear the word of God and keep it!"

Perhaps the most daring single instance we have of Christ's revolutionary attitude toward women is in a set of three parables in Luke 15. They all tell about the desire of God to save sinners. Some people see them as also teaching about the Trinity. In the first story, God is a Shepherd seeking a lost sheep. You know who the Good Shepherd is. In the last story God is the Father of a prodigal son. You know who the good Father is. Do you remember the middle parable? It is a woman seeking a lost coin in a dark house. Is it unreasonable to suppose that the woman represents the Holy Spirit? Anyway, we know that she represents God. All three parables end in rejoicing.

This is not the place to go on describing Christ's many extraordinary examples of regard for women as real people. No. wonder that, as Dorothy Sayers puts it, women were the last at the cross and the first at the tomb.

WHOSE SLAVE ARE YOU?

That brings us back to the good news from Paul to all of us about Jesus: "In Christ Jesus you are all sons of God, through faith. For as many of you as were baptized into Christ have put on Christ. There is neither Jew nor Greek, there is neither slave nor free, there is neither male nor female; for you are all one in Christ Jesus" (Gal. 3: 26-28, RSV).

Paul was naming three divisions that separated people of his day into supposedly superior and inferior groups. First and foremost here, Paul doesn't want Greek Christians to be looked down upon by superior-feeling Jewish Christians. He doesn't want the non-Jews forced into "slavery" to Jewish religious rules such as circumcision. (Greek Christian women were safe on that one.)

Second, Paul doesn't want Christians who are literal slaves to be seen as anything less than fully equal Christian brothers (and you know where that finally leads). We can see how he handles that in his letter to the slave owner Philemon. We are surprised he wasn't more outspoken than he was.

Third, Paul doesn't want females to be looked down on by males or treated as anything less than fully equal Christian sisters. But he never wrote much more about that issue in any of his writings that we have. (Quite the contrary sometimes, it would seem.) He just worked at it in his own life, apparently.

Because Paul didn't go on and develop his case against slave-holding and the subjection of women, some people have held that he approved of them. They have even quoted him in defense of both practices!

For example, in Ephesians 6 Paul told the Christian slaves of his day to serve their masters with perfect diligence and faithfulness. That was good advice for the interim. I am sure that Paul would cheer today because slavery is almost extinct. He would hardly have advised Christian slaves in America to ignore the Emancipation Proclamation (or the Underground Railroad?) and to continue in subjection to their wrongful masters. After all, the faith Paul taught is what eventually, belatedly, killed slavery. (Read Grace Irwin's biography of John Newton, *Servant of Slaves*.)

Slavery and the subjection of women have points in common. Living as he did in the powerful Roman Empire, Paul probably didn't dream that either one would pass away before the return of Christ. I think Paul would cheer now because women are securing more personal identity and social justice today than they have had before. Paul was for Christian maturity and freedom.

In my own opinion, if women had had more enemies like Paul in the past, we wouldn't need so many friends. But social justice will never be complete in this world, and in the meantime Paul's advice to all Christians can be summed up in the popular motto, "Bloom where you are planted."

CHAPTER FIVE

WOMAN'S ROLEPLAY

What Is Woman's Proper Place, and Who's to Put Her in It?

Proverbs 31: 25, 26 (RSV): Strength and dignity are her clothing, and she laughs at the time to come. She opens her mouth with wisdom, and the teaching of kindness is on her tongue.

Proverbs 31: 31 (RSV): Give her of the fruit of her hands, and let her works praise her in the gates.

CHAPTER FIVE

Woman's Roleplay

THAT MAN OVER THERE say that women needs to be helped into carriages, and lifted over ditches, and to have the best place everywhere. Nobody ever helps me into carriages, or over mud puddles, or gives me any best place! And ain't I a woman? Look at me! Look at my arm! I have ploughed and planted and gathered into barns, and no man could head me—and ain't I a woman? I could work as much and eat as much as a man—when I could get it—and bear the lash as well! And ain't I a woman? I have born thirteen children and seen most of 'em sold into slavery and when I cried out with my mother's grief, none but Jesus heard me—and ain't I a woman?"

LADIES AND WOMEN

I pity that minister whose public speech about the weakness and fragility of women caused the above outburst from Sojourner Truth. She was a tall, gaunt ex-slave from New York. His sentimental speech was forgotten 123 years ago, but her unscheduled answer is still being reprinted.

Sojourner Truth was not a fine lady. Most women in the world aren't. And that is probably for the best. In 1941 Sinclair Lewis said, "A 'lady' is a woman so incompetent as to have to take refuge in a secluded class, like kings and idiots, who have to be treated with special kindness because they can't take it." Of course it isn't nice to sneer at incompetent people, but Lewis made his point. What surprises me is that many women are still taught to strive for incompetence in order to be ladylike.

A small Christian periodical recently printed a woman's question asking if she should feel excluded by the term "the sons of God." The male editor answered, "The sons of God is not an exclusive phrase, but it does imply vigilance, strength, fighting, warriorship, etc., and we should do well to leave it that way. Then too, why should women want to be men, or ladies gentlemen? God created them the way they are, and that, dear lady, is one reason why men like them." Could he have read Galatians 3: 26-28?

Why the "dear lady" received such an unwarranted rebuke puzzled me, and I had the feeling that this editor was a frustrated grandson of the very minister who preached to Sojourner Truth about being a lady. I can imagine what she might reply if she were alive today. She was a good fighter.

I remember my own first public appearance. I was almost three, very shy, and I had been taken to Sunday school a few times by country neighbors. My parents came to the Christmas program to see me recite my piece alone on the stage. I remember a vague flurry of angel wings and a large gold star. Then my turn came.

"The star shines bright and I don't fight," I piped perfectly. Before anyone could say the next part, I added loudly, "But that's what I want to do!"

I was the gentlest of little girls; I suppose that I had accidentally added part of someone else's piece to my own. But my addition was prophetic. I have had to fight for several things in my life, including my faith and my sanity. Thank God that I wanted to!

Woman's Roleplay

HOUSEWIFE IS NOT ENOUGH

Thirty years later I was still capable of embarrassing myself in public by not sticking to the expected words. Once I attended a meeting of bright, lively, full-time housewives, mostly Christians, who were being addressed by a professional home economist. She began by raising the bugaboo of the "just a housewife" syndrome and waved it away with the "expert homemaker" concept. Today the term has graduated to "home executive"—but the pay is the same.

Then our speaker asked for a show of hands of those who found the role of homemaker entirely satisfying in itself. All of the women affably raised their hands. All but me. I was thinking. Then she asked for all who felt that they needed more than homemaking in their lives for complete fulfillment to raise their hands. All alone, my hand went halfway up.

Only later did it occur to me that our home economist hadn't raised her hand at all. How could she? She was a wife and mother working full time at an outside job she really liked. (She didn't have to work.) And part of her job, she felt, was to encourage happy full-time homemaking.

So she listed all the professional aspects of a homemaker's role: interior decorator, gourmet cook, chauffeur, sanitary engineer, financier, child psychologist, nurse, fashion designer, ecologist, chemist, efficiency expert, nutritionist, receptionist, hostess, and general manager. This argument always fails to impress me. In fact, it depresses me because it insults my intelligence. If I am reasonably satisfied as a full-time homemaker it is not because of delusions about professional status.

HIGH-STATUS HOME EXECUTIVES

I remember reading about a handsome and lovable retarded boy who will probably never be able to support himself in adulthood. Someone said that a girl with his capacities would have a brighter future because she could make a good little wife and mother. Some profession!

During the Second World War when hired help was almost impossible to get, some wag put an ad in a national magazine that catered to intellectuals. He offered the services of highly trained chimpanzees to do basic housecleaning and to serve as maids. The joke was on him; he received a small flood of requests from readers who took him seriously.

I read a beautifully written article once about gleaming oven racks. The author had retired from a budding career as a writer to become the wife of a professional man and the mother of a darling baby or two. She rhapsodized about the pleasures of sunning pillows and sewing curtains. She advised educated women to forget their former interests entirely and enjoy pure homemaking. Her husband brought her an armful of daffodils on a gray day, I recall, and brought exciting friends home to dinner.

If I had a hired chimpanzee to help, my own pillows might get hung out in the sun and my oven racks would always gleam; but, alas, I don't get that far into pure homemaking. (Incidentally, I wouldn't get an armful of daffodils if I did.) But I felt less guilty when it occurred to me that this reformed writer had still managed to get her article written and published in one of the world's finest newspapers. For any young woman that is no mean accomplishment. I'm sure it pleased her no end.

CHRISTIAN AUTHORITY

There are many Christian (as well as non-Christian) authorities who claim that all women should stay in the home full time, and they have two main reasons. First is that women are too mentally or physically weak to really qualify for anything else. They may *seem* to qualify, but evil will come of it. The other reason is that homemaking is so challenging and/or difficult that only the full efforts of a gifted woman can do it justice. Take your choice and bite the bullet.

One of Christianity's greatest, most colorful teachers was Martin Luther. He claimed that men, having broad shoulders and narrow hips, accordingly possess intelligence. Women have narrow shoulders and broad hips. Therefore women should stay home, sit on their wide buttocks, keep house, and bear and raise children. (I don't see what keeping house and rearing children have in common with sitting.) When Martin Luther encountered Copernicus' novel theory that the earth orbits the sun, he responded, "This fool wishes to reverse the entire scheme of astronomy. But sacred Scripture tells us Joshua commanded the sun to stand still, not the earth." I enjoy a man who errs in heroic proportions when he errs.

Another one of our most endearing and colorful Christian writers, G. K. Chesterton, answered the charge that the ordinary woman is a drudge with a reminder that the ordinary man is hardly a cabinet minister. At least running a house is in some small degree creative and individual. A housewife isn't following orders all day like her husband. (His wife had no children.)

Chesterton wanted women to find a magnificent outlet for creativity in the kitchen. "Let her invent, if she likes, a new dish every day of her life," he suggested. "So far from wishing her to get cooked meals from outside, I should like her to cook more wildly." He suggested that woman has enough occasion for bravery in the bedroom and adventure in the kitchen to totally fill her life.

When I suggested this to some female friends of mine, they said that adventure in the bedroom and bravery in the kitchen sounded more appropriate today, especially when you consider the constant risk of throwing another wild new hamburger casserole down the garbage disposal because the kids won't eat it. That would be especially brave at today's prices. I don't know just what Chesterton meant about woman's bravery in the bedroom, but it is a fact that he was married in Victorian England to a reportedly neurotic, frigid, and frail woman; and he weighed 300 pounds.

In a nation of rather small men, Chesterton was a giant in more ways than one. But he wasn't too keen on women getting the vote. As he saw it, politics was not part of a woman's job.

GETTING OUR JOBS DONE

One morning my son Jonathan refused to go to kindergarten. In fact, he said he would never go there again. I knew that kindergarten work was really hard for him and that he was discouraged. So I tried to show him that we all have our jobs that we have to do, and his job was to go to school. I became dramatic.

"What if I decided not to cook or sew or clean house anymore? What if I wouldn't wash clothes or make the beds! What kind of mother would I be?"

"A rich mother," he shot back instantly.

Jonathan may have trouble in school, but he has a canny streak in him. I've been thinking about that answer for five years now.

When I hear a famous Christian claim that woman's highest calling is to be a housewife, I wonder first of all about the women who have to support themselves. In our church there are some housewives who have regular cleaning women to do much of their work for them. Is the cleaning woman performing God's highest calling for women? Or is scrubbing the floor a sacred duty only for women poor enough to have to scrub their own floor but not poor enough to have to scrub someone else's?

And what of the rich housewives? (Housewives are paid

according to their husbands' degree of success, not according to the quality of their own homemaking. I wonder how that makes rich housewives feel.) Is hiring expensive interior decorators and planning trips to the Bahamas and Hawaii and getting the Cadillac washed and collecting valuable antiques God's highest calling for those women? I have never heard a famous Christian say what he means by housewife.

Actually, I have hired help now too. I have recently started paying Jonathan to do some simple tasks for me six days a week. He is only ten years old, but in his slapdash way he is quite helpful. Although Jonathan is male, I feel that vacuuming the carpet is a higher calling for him this year than it is for me.

LOYALTY OATH

Don't misunderstand me. I like being a housewife. There are three concrete reasons why I know how much I like it.

First, for six years I taught high school, five classes a day, 36 pupils to a class. I taught in spike heels on concrete floors because our male principal considered these painful shoes more ladylike. I not only prepared nightly lesson plans and weekly tests for each subject (I usually taught two subjects), but I also had to grade and record the 180 tests. That was easier than correcting the 180 themes I collected every week. This was just my weekly routine, not to mention the mountains of secretarial work, quarterly grading, disciplinary actions, teachers' meetings, parent conferences, chaperoning assignments, lunch patrol, and other jobs. (All summer I worked on visual aids and other classroom enrichment as well as studying literature.) It seemed as if I hardly had any time for my own thoughts from 6:30 A. M. when I got up until 1:00 A. M. when I collapsed back into bed. I was never paid for half the hours I worked. In fact, I started at about $3,000 a year and quit at about $7,000.

ON MY WAY UP FROM EDEN

When people complain, "Why don't kids learn any English in school?" I sigh deeply. I knew some who did.

The wonderful thing that happened when I quit teaching to become a full-time homemaker (I had been a homemaker all along) was that I could go barefoot and my mind finally had time to relax. Women complain that housewives are mentally unemployed. That's not all bad!

A busy housewife can pray off and on all day long. She can practice loving people mentally. She can sneak in some reading or listen to records and cassette recordings while she works. She can listen to important thoughts and ideas that well up quietly in her mind. Some of my most exciting communion with God has come when I am drying dishes or changing sheets. I didn't have time to communicate that way with God when I was out in public. I was too frazzled.

Perhaps I wouldn't have grown into it yet if it hadn't been for the serious illness which taught me to stop and live more fully. That illness, which occurred shortly after I quit teaching, is the second reason why I know I like housekeeping. There was no assurance that I would ever be able to hang out clothes or cook a meal or dust a room again. I had a condition that seemed like creeping polio. It lasted for months. Since then I consciously enjoy the feeling of textures and pressures under my feet, the delight of stretching to reach something, and the joy of being able to hurry around the house. How I thank God for the physical freedom not only to use the bathtub again, but to be able to scrub it.

Right now I have an extra mess to clean up every day. It is a layer of pulpy pink and brown flowers constantly dropping onto my driveway and front walk. They are slippery and dirty and hard to clean up, and I get tired of them. Then I remember to look up to the reason they are there. A gigantic bouquet of hundreds of orchidlike flowers shines above me against the sky. Our silk floss tree is abloom again. It is the highlight of the fall for me.

Woman's Roleplay

This brings me to the third reason I know I am glad to be a housewife. Sometimes I get discouraged with the endless cycle of dirty fingerprints and torn pajamas and muddy shoes and stolen bicycles. Then I try to remember to look up at the shining reasons for all the mess—the very highlights of my life.

BEYOND THE SUNSET MAGAZINES

A few weeks after the depressing home economics meeting, I read Betty Friedan's book *The Feminine Mystique* and felt much better. She says that women need to have an identity and vocation, using their talents aside from their husbands and children. She says that the homemaking routine is simply not enough for most women. Homemaking alone is a dead end.

It is true. Husband and children, good food and a beautiful home. Dead end. That is what Christ keeps telling us, anyway. There has to be more than these well-filled barns.

My favorite indoor household task is interior decorating. I like art. But ever since I admired an especially charming house one day which was swept away the next day by a sudden flood, I have had less interest in our furnishings. I don't claim to be unworldly; I keep our house pleasant. But I realize that our house is built upon sand in that we happen to live in earthquake territory. And, in another sense, all the earth is earthquake territory now. What use is there in refeathering our summer nests over and over when we think we feel fall breezes stirring? It seems to me that really interior furnishing is what counts today.

"Man may work from sun to sun, but woman's work is never done." Housekeeping is a task that swells to fill every moment a woman will give to it. (The women who give it 20 hours a day get institutionalized.) Each woman has to decide where to cut it off. For years I turned the collars and cuffs on all my husband's shirts and almost doubled their wear that way. Fortunately shirts are now made so that the collars can't be turned. I was a diehard about ironing pillowcases, but I finally gave it up as a vice.

My family goes dessertless most of the time, and it doesn't hurt us a bit. It saves time and money and cuts down on empty calories. When I want to spend extra time in the kitchen, I tend to make a pitcher of fresh carrot juice rather than a cake. (Nix on mixes.) Instead of the gourmet cooking that G. K. Chesterton (all 300 pounds of him) recommended to women, I hope to move steadily toward simpler meals and good plain nutrition. It's a matter of stewardship. (If cooking were my "gift," that would be different. I have a friend who ministers to others that way.)

MONKEY BUSINESS

I remember a magazine story about a bride who could not please her finicky husband with her cooking. Her magnificent strawberry shortcake was not like his mother's. Her delicious attempts at spaghetti were never like his mom's. One day in a fit of frustration, she went shopping for clothes, had a couple of drinks, and came home just in time to heat a can of spaghetti for supper. "That's it!" he beamed. "My mother's recipe!"

That reminds me of a friend who married after receiving her B. A. in home economics. On the honeymoon she fixed her first meal for her husband. The fresh-cooked spinach tasted quite strange and terrible. My friend had learned all kinds of fancy "home economics" in college, but she never learned the difference between spinach and romaine lettuce.

— Once my sister was hired to teach home economics at a Roman Catholic boarding school for girls in Kenya. There was no planned curriculum. The girls were from dirt-floor huts. My sister taught them to embroider tea towels.

Much of what passes for homemaking in our culture is monkey business. I made that decision after a few years of dutifully doing things like decorating soap with decals and copying useless recipes and reading most of the advertisements that came in the mail. I decided it the day I absolutely refused to take a course in cake-decorating. It was an exhilarating experience. I'm not at all against cake-decorating or other monkey business, you understand, but this monkey wants to choose her own business. I have had many occasions to be devoutly thankful that I never developed my dormant cake-decorating talent. I will take that talent to the grave with me unused.

A housewife may or may not be an expert homemaker, but she should be liberated. She should spend her time doing her own kind of valuable, loving things for herself and others. She should keep house without the house keeping her. And she should be liberated from the constant danger of narrow, self-centered living in her own small family world.

THE HEART OF HOMEMAKING

A physician once said, "One only loves those whom one serves." I think the reason most girls still hope to marry and raise families (in contrast to the eloquent young movie actress who said recently, "Who wants all that garbage with babies and wives and husbands and junk like that?") is because of their desire to love and to serve with love.

That may be one reason why so few women develop their intellect. Society almost says they will be better wives and mothers if they stay feminine and a little dumb. That is the belief of Nina Braunwald, who is an unusual wife and mother.

"My career as a cardiac surgeon is my luxury," Dr. Braunwald said when accepting an academic honor, "my hobby, my reward, my extravagance, and I do not permit it to use up my psychological energy or to leave me too tired to do the duties of the home." Dr. Braunwald surmounted great odds and became the first woman to be elected to membership in the exclusive American Association of Thoracic Surgeons.

She reminds me of a charming and fluttery woman I knew who would exclaim, "I am so glad the Bible makes men the leaders in everything! We women don't have the brains to understand complicated things." Her husband is a highly successful middle-aged Christian businessman. If he ever has to have heart surgery, I hope he will have a surgeon as expert as Nina Braunwald.

One well-known handbook for Christian living lists as *point one* for the responsibility of a wife: "Stay home where you belong." The Biblical reference given to prove the point is: "Train the young women to love their husbands and children, to be sensible, chaste, domestic, kind, and submissive to their husbands" (Titus 2: 4, 5, RSV). I don't see the connection. From what I read about our cardiac surgeon, she seems loving, sensible, chaste, domestic, kind, and submissive to her husband. Why not?

THE SPICE OF LIFE

Variety of life-styles is increasing. A young professional woman recently told me that she is looking for a job in Oregon, her home state, but that she will settle for one in northern California if she has to. Knowing that her husband is in the computer business here, I was afraid that she meant that their marriage was breaking up.

"What about Steve?" I asked hesitantly. She explained that although she loves her profession, he wants out of his. He has a consuming new interest in photography. When they move north, she will support the two of them and he will spend his time at home learning the art and technology of photography. (I heard of a divorced man who snarls into the telephone, "I *am* the lady of the house!") I think that my friend is loving, sensible, chaste, domestic, kind, and submissive. I also think she is smart.

A couple of other smart friends of mine quit their successful careers when the first baby came in order to spend all their time taking care of their young families. They have both confided to me that they feel almost a bit guilty about happily staying at home, tending their families, getting plenty of rest, and letting the rest of the world go by. In my opinion, the rest of the world would go by much more smoothly if it were blessed with many mothers like these two. My friend the wise young professor, said once, "Availability to everybody is availability to nobody." I liked that almost as well as his Mobius Strip. Each person has to choose how far his availability will spread and where it needs to be channeled.

Sometimes the choice is made for us. I remember meeting Alice Cooper once. Not the frowzy male rock star, but a sprightly little woman 90 years old in Pennsylvania. Her husband had died suddenly around 1900, leaving her to run their farm and rear six children alone. She did it all successfully and lived to 96. The weaker sex indeed.

I have a friend who has discovered (now that her children are nearing adulthood) that when she stays home, although active and happy, her blood pressure goes up. When she exercises her special gifts and training outside the home five days a week, even as a volunteer, her blood pressure returns to normal. Knowing this, her husband would push her out the door if she didn't go of her own accord.

Harry Truman used to say, "If you can't stand the heat, get out of the kitchen." In contrast, Senator Barry Goldwater said that he has nothing against a female Vice President so long as she still cooks dinner and gets home on time. I didn't find that very funny. And neither would the extremely gifted older couple I know who have always left the cooking to the husband because he enjoys it and she doesn't. (I wouldn't want to guess who does the cleanup.)

I have read of another working couple who didn't get along well right after returning home from work. So they switched to a schedule in which the husband gave the wife an hour at home alone to refresh herself so that she could welcome him home "after a hard day's work." Then everything came up roses.

THE FACTS, MA'AM

No matter what *point one* is for wives in a handbook, the fact is that nine out of ten women today go to work outside the home sooner or later. Half of them have to. How do they work and run a house at the same time?

The average woman who works eight hours a day outside trims two hours a day from her housework, according to one survey. She does that by being more efficient, leaving less important tasks undone, buying helpful appliances, or hiring some help if she can afford it. Some employed wives spend as little as three and a half hours a day on housework in contrast to a high of 12 hours a day for unemployed mothers of extra-large families.

Mothering may be a woman's most important career, but millions of women are never mothers. And for those who are, it can hardly take over 25 years at the most. If a healthy woman fulfilled her biological potential for reproducing to the utmost, she could bear 20 or 30 children and really fill her life with child care. I haven't heard anyone recommend that!

The typical woman today enters school at five and marries at 19. Before she is 35 her last child enters school and she has time alone at home. She also has more than half her lifetime ahead of her! When she is 45 her last child graduates from high school. In 1900 this typical woman would have conveniently died at 48, and we would be done with her. But today she has another 25 or 30 years to while away.

One-tenth of women today do manage to pass all those

years without working. But the rest of the women average 25 years of employment, many taking time out for child-rearing. The average single woman works 45 years (two years longer than the average male), in spite of narrow shoulders, wide hips, and all.

OUT OF HER PLACE

Women have descended to working in the coal mines now. One woman in rural Pennsylvania who had been doing housework for $10 a day went into mining so that she could better support her eight children. She makes about $42 a day there. It's hard work, but she claims that it is no harder than scrubbing and waxing floors. I think that none of the male coal miners can speak with authority on the comparison.

It isn't easy for women to find their way or fight their way into these high-paying jobs. One woman with 152 IQ and an Oxford M. A. tried her luck with Los Angeles employment agencies and found that all she qualified for was to be a receptionist for about $550 a month. Fortunately, she didn't really need the job.

In contrast, I read of a beautiful young college graduate who sincerely wanted to be a carpenter. After being turned down for the apprenticeship program in Pittsburgh, she went to Switzerland and spent a year as an apprentice. Then she returned to Pittsburgh and tried again. The union officials said she failed the written examination required of all applicants. That seems unlikely in light of the fact that she has a B. A. with honors in English. She is taking her case to court.

In my city we have a female roofer. She and her young husband work on top of houses together!

I met a young woman last year who answered my questions about becoming a doctor. Her father is a surgeon and the family is active in a Christian group that emphasizes medical training. She received top grades in college in a pre-med course. After graduation she studied and toured in Europe to make sure that she knew her own mind. She was sure.

When the admissions director at the Christian medical school interviewed her, he said, "Do you realize that if we take you here, you will be crowding out some young man who will eventually have a family to support?" (I didn't know that supporting a family made a person a superior physician.) Her record was so good that they had to take her anyway.

Now that she is being forced to choose a specialty in order to finish, she thinks she will go into pediatrics. She would prefer to work with people of all ages, but she isn't sure how much longer she can go on absorbing all the friendly jokes and unfriendly digs and sexual overtures. (She is a slight wisp of a girl with fair skin and long blonde hair, and she looks about 17 years old.) "Babies don't see me as a freak," she sighed.

Since I talked with her I learned that the suicide rate for United States women physicians is three times that for women in general. And they tend to commit suicide younger. I'd say it's no wonder.

JUST CALCULATING

In our culture the bias against women doctors is similar to the curious assumption that girls are inferior at math. I learned early that math is for boys, and yet I always got higher grades in math than the boys in my classes. That was uncomfortable, and I soon came to dislike the subject. (Another reason I disliked math was that when I asked really exciting questions about numerical relationships and processes, the teachers acted flustered and angry and never answered. I suspect that New Math answers some of those questions; I was born too soon.) Algebra and geometry were fun, but I took them only because I absolutely had to, and then I quit math forever. I intended to be feminine.

Woman's Roleplay

Our large adult Sunday school class elects new officers every six months. Once, for fun, we switched sex roles and elected a male secretary and a female treasurer. It made for a great deal of hilarity and high spirits for six months. What most of the class members probably don't know is that two of the prettiest little housewives in the class have master's degrees in math. They are my personal friends. I don't happen to know any men who majored in math.

"There has never been a great mathematical genius who was a woman." That claim may well be true. It could no doubt be made for some other groups also. But how can we be sure, in light of the fact that the greatest mathematical genius we do know of was almost undiscovered. He was a peasant boy in India who had no books, and so he figured out about 3,000 years worth of mathematical discoveries all by himself. Some English people discovered him and sent him to Cambridge where his genius was confirmed and where he promptly picked up some English germ and died.

It makes me wonder how many peasant girls have lived and died and taken their genius with them. It reminds me of William Wordsworth's sentimental tribute to Lucy, an unknown country girl who died young.

> She dwelt among the untrodden ways
> Beside the springs of Dove:
> A maid whom there were none to praise
> And very few to love.

PROFESSIONAL ADVICE

William Wordsworth's friend, the successful poet Robert Southey, advised a quiet country spinster named Charlotte Bronte to live like Lucy instead of trying to write. He told her, "Literature cannot be the business of a woman's life, and it ought not to be. The more she is engaged in her proper duties, the less leisure will she have for it, even as an accomplishment and a recreation."

I assume that proper duties for a spinster included embroidering tea towels and cake-decorating. Southey's advice reminds me of the saying I heard when I was a child, that whistling girls and crowing hens always come to no-good ends. (I quit whistling for a week or two.)

Charlotte didn't take Southey's advice and, sure enough, she eventually died. (So did Southey.)

Now, over a century later, Robert Southey's writings are almost totally forgotten, but the Bronte sisters' novels *Jane Eyre* and *Wuthering Heights* look good for another century or two at least.

It's hard for men like Southey to keep women like Bronte in their place. As a Russian proverb says, "Easier to manage a sackful of fleas than one woman." That brings us to the question of power.

CHAPTER SIX

WOMAN'S POWER PLAY

What Power Should Women Wield, and What Power Should They Yield?

I John 5: 1-5 (RSV): Every one who believes that Jesus is the Christ is a child of God, and every one who loves the parent loves the child. By this we know that we love the children of God, when we love God and obey his commandments. For this is the love of God, that we keep his commandments. And his commandments are not burdensome. For whatever is born of God overcomes the world; and this is the victory that overcomes the world, our faith. Who is it that overcomes the world but he who believes that Jesus is the Son of God?

II Timothy 1: 7 (RSV): God did not give us a spirit of timidity but a spirit of power and love and self-control.

CHAPTER SIX

Woman's Power Play

THE MOST OUTRAGEOUS MODERN STORY I ever read was about a pitiful man whose wife could always outdo him. It went roughly like this: Altha beat George in everything from tennis to chess. She could drink him under the table and manage their business better than he could. She was bigger and louder and smarter and stronger and braver.

Eventually a gentle young woman named Peggy came to live with them. Naturally, George fell in love with Peggy, and he felt that her quiet smiles indicated that she loved him too. He finally managed to screw up his frail courage to tell his tough wife that he was leaving her for Peggy. He choked out the fact that he was leaving and got no farther.

"Fine!" Altha interrupted heartily. "Peggy and I are in love and were going to leave you anyway."

I don't recall the author or title of that story, but I should. It strikes a raw nerve today. (It was written before the present women's liberation movement began.) I think it points up a latent fear which sets many men against women's rights.

CRAZY WALTER

The most outrageous *old* story I ever read is the story of

Patient Griselda. It was a popular tale in Europe in the Middle Ages. Petrarch and Boccaccio recorded it in Italy around 1350, and Chaucer retold it in England in about 1390.

In Chaucer's version, called "The Clerk's Tale," Lord Walter was urged to marry. On his wedding day he announced his choice of a bride: a poor but exceedingly pure girl he had noticed. She was, of course, beautiful. She became his virtuous queen and bore him a daughter.

Then Walter told her that he needed to dispose of the baby because it was the wrong sex, and a rough servant carried it off to die. Griselda, meek as a lamb, never protested. She lived to please her husband.

Four years later she gave birth to a boy. When he was two, Walter told her that the adorable child would have to die because he was descended from commoners on her side and unfit to inherit the throne. Griselda merely answered that his pleasure was her command, and that was the end of her son.

Six years later Walter told his perfect wife that he was divorcing her and marrying a girl of high estate. He sent her home in disgrace to her poor father. She never complained. Later he called upon her to clean the palace in her rags in preparation for his wedding. She did so sweetly. Her only request was that Walter might not kill the children of his new bride because, being highborn, the girl might not be able to bear such sorrow.

Walter was finally satisfied. He revealed to Griselda that his "new bride" was their 12-year-old daughter. Her eight-year-old brother had come back also. Griselda had passed all three tests—two pretended murders and a most cruel divorce—and now the family could live together in peace and joy. Griselda had proved herself patient and submissive.

Since the story is written in 1,212 lines of Middle English poetry ("It were ful hard to fynde now-a-dayes, In al a town Grisildis thre or two") anyone who reads it through in the original demonstrates quite a bit of patience also.

Woman's Power Play

The moral of the story, perhaps as Petrarch told it, was that Griselda is an example of how we should all accept suffering and trials. Since Petrarch had to live through the horrors of the Black Death, he might have meant it. The less pious Chaucer tacked on a saucy ending from a fictitious woman, warning wives never to be docile like Griselda, but to answer back and defend themselves. Large strong wives don't have to take any nonsense, she attested. And small wives can depend upon their tongues, their beauty, or their friends for protection. Prudent wives will all manage to get the upper hand in one way or another.

THE LOWER HAND

I personally consider both of the above stories outrageous, but there are people in America today who would consider one or the other just right.

A very common Crazy-Walter type joke in our own day is about the farmer who took his bride home in a wagon. The horse stumbled, and he said, "That's once!" Later the horse stumbled again, and he said, "That's twice!" When the horse stumbled a third time, he got out and shot it dead in its harness. The shocked bride cried out in protest, and the farmer said, "That's once."

That reminds me of the Russian proverb: "A dog is wiser than a woman; he won't bark at his master."

Some of these jokes and stories are only bravado, but men really have had the upper hand most of the time through history simply because they are bigger and stronger than women. And during women's strongest years, they are usually tied down with bearing and caring for children. A lot of history is summed up in the motto: "Keep them barefoot and pregnant."

One angry radical liberationist today claims that "the battle of the sexes" is a misnomer; historically it has been a massacre. Over a century ago the Christian abolitionist and feminist Sarah Grimke explained mildly, "I ask no favors for our sex . . . . All I ask of our brethren is that they will take their feet from off our necks."

A favorite answer to such dissatisfied women is: "The hand that rocks the cradle is the hand that rules the world." It's a good line, but it doesn't happen to make any sense when you think about it. (It's not a Bible verse.) The idea is that women who rear children can rule the world through them. I suppose the late Hannah Nixon is supposed to have ruled the world through her son Richard.

First, what of all the women who have no children? Second, what of all the women whose children are themselves female? Third, the only present ruler of this world that I know of is Satan, anyway.

When that poetic line about cradles was written, women's hands were not yet allowed to cast ballots. ("What do women want iv rights whin they have priv'leges?" said Mr. Dooley.) So far as I can see, the hand that rocks the cradle is simply the hand that rocks the cradle. Today the hand that governs India is the hand that governs India. Both are important hands, but it is silly to confuse them.

WHERE DO WE STAND?

The second standard answer to women's request for social equality is that behind every great man there stands a woman. You can hardly dispute that, since even bachelors were born once (remember Dag Hammarskjold?). It is also true that behind every dreadful man there stands a woman (remember Hitler?). Neither statement has much to do with the fact that all women are people in their own right.

I have heard Ruth Graham used repeatedly as a shining example of how women should stay in the home and devote their energies to sustaining a domestic haven for their husbands in order to enable the men to achieve greatness. Woman as facilitator. That sounds especially sensible for women who are married to men with great gifts or special callings. To be a Mrs. Graham or Mrs. Peale or Mrs. Tournier would be quite a career. All three of these women have taken some part in their husbands' careers apart from homemaking, however.

On the other hand, both Abraham Lincoln and John Wesley made terrible marriages, and it didn't hinder their greatness at all. They got along without the comfort of facilitators. Wesley's wife was a nurse who ambushed him when he was weak with illness, and she never gave him any peace or happiness. She probably wasn't even a Christian. Everyone has already heard about Mrs. Lincoln and how miserable she made her husband. It happens that C. S. Lewis was burdened at home for most of his adult life with an atheistic "foster mother" who was every bit as bad as Mrs. Wesley and Mrs. Lincoln. But she didn't keep him from his calling either. Who knows what Billy Graham would be like if he had made a bad marriage; perhaps God could have used him anyway.

One thing we do know: most good wives are not standing behind great men. They are standing behind (or next to) normal men.

TWO KINDS OF MARRIAGE

Christians who believe that wives should be subservient to their husbands surely don't mean to impose that ideal upon non-Christians who choose to enter a marriage that is a partnership rather than a hierarchy. (We're lucky if non-Christians marry at all anymore.) Actually, some Christian marriages are partnerships and some are hierarchical; some non-Christian marriages are partnerships and some are hierarchical. And most are a mixture.

In our democratic society, partnership and compromise and arbitration are easier to understand. Hierarchy, which used to be the rule throughout life, is a bit mysterious today, at least to Protestants. I recently met a handsome, athletic young man who spent a year at an Evangelical seminary and then went looking for a Christian community to join for life. After visiting several Protestant groups, he was living at a Benedictine monastery as a working "observer." If he decides to stay, he will convert to Roman Catholicism and go through the steps to become a monk!

In response to my questions, he explained that he spent all his young life in complete freedom from rules in a nominally Christian home. Now he felt that he needed a totally structured adult life for balance. For him this might mean voluntary submission to monastic rule and to a monastic superior as God's representative to him. It isn't only women who sometimes choose utter submission to others as God's answer for their particular lives.

All Christians receive a kind of power through submitting to God. Some people also receive a kind of peace from submitting to human authorities.

SHADES OF GRISELDA

I think of Christian friends of mine who recently joined an authoritarian Christian community which specializes in seminars for women and teaches rigid hierarchy as God's way for all of us. My friends obey the founder implicitly because he is supposed to be God's only prophet since Paul. He claims to be an Evangelical who has received special revelation.

Many of his rules are about femininity and masculinity. A woman must never wear wool clothing or short hair. (If her hair won't grow long, she has to buy a wig.) Girls must not wear trousers. (Especially displeasing to God are any women's pants that zip down the front or have flared legs.)

Women are to wear lace, flowers, and romantic dresses.

More important, the wife is to obey her husband exactly as Patient Griselda did; she can never object to anything he does. (Forget the Nuremberg trials.) Each child must obey the child who was born before him, and the oldest child obeys the mother. When I asked about twins or retarded children, they said the leader hadn't revealed that to them yet.

The rules go on to cover many aspects of life. Free enterprise is God-ordained. Adoption of children is wrong. Single women must live in subjection to their fathers or else must seek some other male such as an employer as a substitute. Men must obey their employers as Christ. I will not go into the more bizarre matters I have heard.

This is not the Children of God sect, remember. I think it draws mainly from middle-aged Christians who are tired or troubled. My friends have really achieved some improved health and well-being under this regime.

FEMININE WILES

A less radical, more widespread feminine movement for Christian women tells them to keep their fingernails clean and stresses pink ruffles and curls and pouting and flirting. No proficiency or higher education is permitted. The Christian woman is to be a flouncy little girl who stamps her feet and bats her eyes and thereby melts a man's heart and gets her way. It takes concentrated practice at first, but the investment is supposed to pay off handsomely.

The game playing has to go on even when there isn't a man within 50 miles to observe her or help her. She must never pound nails, fix faucets, carry big boxes, or, I suppose, save her child if he were pinned under a fallen tree. Women must be frilly and helpless if they want to get favors from men.

All of this is based upon veneration of a minor character in a Dickens novel whom he called a "child-bride." The fact is that Dickens never said he liked her; in fact, he made her die young so that the hero became free to go on to maturity. I assume that no one who takes the course has ever really read Dickens. Nevertheless, some Christian women say their marriages have been revitalized since they stopped nagging and started flouncing. I don't doubt it.

A similar nationwide seminar on femininity for Christian wives stresses the importance of making husbands happy by building their egos and thrilling them sexually. The leader is quoted as promising, "He in turn will gratefully respond by trying to make it up to her and grant her desires. He may even want to spoil her with goodies." The latter is all we need!

I have nothing at all against sexual thrills or curls and lace. But it seems ironic that these manipulation teachers also stress that the man has to be the absolute ruler in the marriage. In my opinion, it is time to paraphrase a rule Christ gave us about male-female relationships. "You have heard it said that it is a sin for a woman to rule over her husband. But I say that when a woman tries to manipulate her husband she has committed the sin of ruling him already in her heart."

THE POWER GRAB

We are all tempted to manipulate others. Where does an honest request become a command, and where does influence become manipulation? Many a woman who pays lip service to male authority has a hard time working it out in real life, and so do some men.

I know a single woman who has had her dates challenge her to submit to sexual overtures on the basis of Bible teachings about male authority. (Unfortunately for them, she understands her Bible better than they do.) I know a married woman whose employer, the principal of a popular Christian school, warned her not to resign her job until he gave her permission to do so, since women are not to usurp authority. (He also offered her children free tuition as an enticement to keep her on, but she told me she wouldn't send her children to such a shoddy school if he doubled her salary to get them there.) It really bothered her to be accused of being unsubmissive (sinful) when she refused to renew her contract.

In contrast to such scruples, one devout wife felt she absolutely had to get her house carpeted before a special occasion. So she had it done as a surprise for her husband because she knew that if she consulted him first he would veto the project. By moving fast, she got her carpet and avoided disobeying her husband, she figured. After all, once it was laid he could fuss and fume, but he couldn't command her not to buy it.

The following monologue is in almost the exact words of one frustrated widow. (I wrote it down as soon as she finished talking to me.)

I said to Don, "*You're* the head of our home! Now get in there and tell the man you want to buy his property!" We entered and stood before the terrible old man. Don said nothing.

The old man finally said, "What do you two want here?" I held my tongue. Don was struck mute as usual.

The old man said, "Speak up or get out of here!" So I told him that we had come to ask to buy his property. He let us buy it.

God knows I didn't want to run the business. But as years went by, Don lost interest in it completely. At closing time he just went home and left me there to do all the finances after waiting on customers and running the machines all day. He finally quit going in at all and tried to sell insurance, which he failed at. He blamed me for getting him into business in the first place. It had been all his idea, but I just said, "Yes, dear, I was mistaken. I'm sorry."

All I wanted was to be a Christian homemaker and helpmeet for Don the way the Bible says for women. But every time I entered the hospital, he signed some fool contract or made some terrible business mistake, and finally we lost everything we had worked and slaved for all those years. Bankruptcy. Within a year of that Don died of heart failure.

Now I am a widow working in an office to support myself and our younger son. I sure hope to get married again soon. I have two requirements for my next husband. He has to be born again, and he has to have at least $10,000.

My older son became a homosexual. I don't know how it happened. Please pray for him.

God have mercy upon both her poor sons. And upon all high-strung women married to low-strung men. A lot of good it did for the Church to tell Don to be the real leader in that house. It might as well have told him to become an astronaut. Thank goodness he is becoming a great success in Life now.

It's a fact that some women have a lot more psychic energy (for good or evil) than their husbands. If such husbands popped "uppers" and their wives popped "downers," they would fit the Church's marriage pattern better. There might be just a grain of truth in Kipling's nasty statement that the silliest woman can manage a clever man, but it takes a very clever woman to manage a fool.

WHICH PANTS?

"Who wears the pants in your family?" a new friend asked my husband. There was a very long thoughtful pause. For me it became a sweaty-hands pause. My femininity and personhood were both on the line.

Finally my husband said, "Neither one of us tells the other

one what to do, if that's what you mean. We just work together cooperatively as mutual helpers, dividing our areas of responsibility. I guess if we ever had an unnegotiable difference I would make the final decision. But that may never happen." (He is a wonderful man.)

I remember the time when I had to make the most painful personal decision of my life, and I simply could not make it because it was the choice between two very terrible alternatives. After consulting our minister and a few other important people, John took the responsibility for the decision upon himself and, in compassionate love, ordered me to obey him. I have bitterly regretted the decision ever since, but I do not regret obeying him. In fact, I even think that he was right, but his rightness is beside the point. Part of living is taking risks, including the risk of being wrong and having to throw oneself upon the grace of God. He took that risk for me.

If John is ever paralyzed by overwhelming circumstances, I trust that I will serve him as he served me. I will make the decision for him that he is unable to make for himself.

"Who wears the pants in your family?" is in the same category as the question, "Have you stopped beating your wife yet?" It is a lying question because it includes a false assumption. Only very ignorant people or very imaginative, caring people who know what they are doing would feel free to ask such a question. Our new friend was one of the latter.

WOMAN AS DANCER

As a child, C. S. Lewis used to have terrible nightmares about insects. He was repulsed by them because they whir and chirp and seem to have all their working parts on the outside. But as an adult he analyzed his dislike for them in terms of society. "In the hive and the ant hill we see fully realized the two things that some of us most dread for our own species—the dominance of the female and the dominance of the collective." No wonder some people thought Lewis disliked women and socialism.

Lewis sincerely believed in the natural authority of husbands over wives, parents over children, and educated over uneducated. He would have liked real patriarchal monarchy. (Never another election; try to imagine that.) But because we are all sinful, none of us should wield the power of a king over others. The natural hierarchy in life has to be hidden behind equal citizenship, Lewis decided. Women should be guaranteed equal political and career and property rights because if men have all the power they will treat women unfairly. Furthermore, Lewis said that in no way should women have to live in servile submission to their husbands.

Lewis believed that there is a constant interchange of services to each other in life. Marriage keeps moving like a dance. We are all constantly teaching and learning, forgiving and being forgiven. "Obedience and rule are more like a dance than a drill—specially between man and woman where the roles are always changing." For a man who hated dancing, Lewis used the image surprisingly often. He liked the *idea* of dancing.

He wrote in *Miracles* that to be high or central means to abdicate continually; to be low means to be raised. (In a good family, isn't the helpless little baby the king?) To Lewis both constant equality and constant inequality seemed flat and unreal. What we want is all the overtones, counterpart, and vibrant sensitiveness of reality.

Only at the end of his life was Lewis himself married. It bore out what he had guessed. He said then that a good wife contains many persons in herself. Joy was in turn his daughter and his mother, his pupil and his teacher, his subject and his sovereign, his comrade, friend, shipmate, and fellow soldier. She was his mistress and his friend, his sister and his brother! All that in three short years of marriage.

Paul Tournier and his wife Nellie were happily married

Woman's Power Play

almost 50 years. Their formula for personal marital happiness included, among other things: (1) unselfish giving to each other, in which everything is shared together from housework to special interests; (2) transparency, in which nothing at all, mental or physical, is hidden; (3) mutual understanding, in which listening, acceptance, and support go both directions; and (4) spiritual foundations, which means submission together to Jesus Christ and dependence upon Him.

There was apparently no power struggle in either the Lewis marriage or the Tournier marriage. All four of these people were brilliant, not only in intellect. They radiated love and dignity. They fully respected themselves and their spouses. We aren't all so fortunate. What can we ordinary Christians with our insecurities and our projections learn from them?

I nominate "Courtesy." Not just surface courtesy, which is the invaluable and often neglected lubricant of family life, but also what I would call "Deep Courtesy." Giving as much of yourself as you know to your spouse, so far as he is able to accept. Receiving with awe as much of himself as he is able to give back to you. (Even if it is not enough to make you happy.) Constantly yielding and asserting, affirming and ministering. The Biblical words are respect and cherish.

It is hardly a mark of Deep Courtesy to let a person destroy you, or to feed his sickness. Deep Courtesy seeks healing. Deep Courtesy is a right sense of the dance. And every couple's dance is different. Just as insults vary from one family to another and can be extremely subtle, so true words and acts of deference vary from one family to another and can be extremely subtle. Hallmark doesn't really say it best. Hilaire Belloc wrote:

> Of Courtesy, it is much less
> Than Courage of Heart or Holiness,
> Yet in my walk it seems to me
> That the Grace of God is in Courtesy.

WOMAN AS OBJECT

When chess champion Bobby Fischer was asked by his church leaders what kind of girls he would like to meet for social dating, he said, "Vivacious, with big busts." Period. So much for one of our deepest and narrowest analytical minds.

For every woman who gets seemingly rewarded for being a sex object or a status object instead of a person (like those in Hugh Hefner's rabbit warren), there are many who get obviously hurt by that attitude gone wild. As C. S. Lewis observed, when a man says he wants a woman right away, the last thing he wants is a woman. He wants his own sexual gratification, not a person.

There is the story of a young man who asked a college girl what she was doing next Saturday night.

"Committing suicide," she answered.

"Then how about Friday?"

I appreciate that joke; it might make a good sermon along with a short Scripture reading to underline the point.

But it makes me sad because it reminds me of my friend Susan, one of the most radiantly gentle girls I ever knew. She had a uniquely beautiful mind and spirit and a bright sense of humor. When she was a freshman in college 12 years ago a young man took her out on a date and strangled her so that he could use her body to enact his sexual fantasies.

He had told someone earlier that day, "I'm going to have a girl tonight." Not a girl. He never had the girl at all. The girl went to be with Jesus, and there is an electric organ in her small church dedicated to her memory. But there is no music on earth equal to Susan's laughter.

If the stupid, sick-minded boy had raped Susan alive, she might never have laughed again anyway; she was that sensitive. If she had dared to press charges, she would have had to undergo humiliating treatment from male policemen (that is changing for the better) and a nightmare of sexual interrogation in court intended to convince the jury that she might have been a willing victim.

The boy's sexual attitudes and history could not be brought into the case. (I suppose that if he is a confirmed rapist, that could prejudice the jury against him.) And even if he were found guilty, the judge would probably give him a wrist-slap sentence. No wonder so few rape victims have tried to protect other women by bringing the guilty to court.

SAUCE FOR THE GANDER

The most dramatically powerless woman is a rape victim. Rape is now our country's fastest growing crime of violence, and that means fast indeed. A few police now act as decoys to catch rapists and take them to court. Some police departments offer self-defense suggestions to women, such as advice to carry a can of hair spray or a nail file in your purse. But hair spray won't help today's rape situation very much.

A group of feminists protested recently when a virtuous wife and mother was sentenced to life in prison (that means five years, I understand) for shooting one of her two rapists. The protestors felt that the victim was being symbolically raped again by an unfair system of justice. The male judge had instructed the jury to totally blot the fact of rape out of their minds when reaching their verdict about the woman's crime. All they could consider was the fact that she was hysterical—not why she was hysterical.

In contrast, I heard of another country where a woman has the legal right to kill her rapist if she can accomplish the feat within an hour of the rape. Small comfort there, in my estimation. But it might make a few rapists think once.

As it is here, what can a raped woman possibly do to capture her assailant for prosecution? If she were strong enough to overcome him without shooting him, she would have been able to fight him off in the first place.

Try to imagine insanely radical feminists who study karate or buy guns going out in pairs to attack lone men on dark streets or in their homes. The victims would be innocent and defenseless men of middle and upper class. Pilots and lawyers and doctors included. They would be stripped and somehow hurt sexually and left unconscious with need for medical and psychiatric care. No murders, of course.

Even if this were done at the rate of one victim a day in the United States it would be a small fraction of the rate of female rape. But I think it would create such an uproar from men and women that all the law enforcement agencies would spring into action. As a result, perhaps women would finally be better protected from rape when men moved to protect themselves from it. (You notice the relative rarity of skyjacking and kidnapping?)

God forbid such an evil program. But it seems less evil than the present easygoing state of affairs. I hear lots of Christian outcry against dirty pictures, but I have never heard a Christian outcry against rape statistics, the dirtiest picture of all.

"The old maid looks under her bed at night for fear she'll never find a man hiding there," someone said with a wink. I won't wink back. Furthermore, I may take a course in judo.

NEVER UNDERESTIMATE THE POWER

When I was a freshman in college, I began doing daily exercises to get good muscle tone. My roommate, soft and willowy, would have none of it.

"I don't want strong muscles," she declared. "All I want out of life is to get married and have babies. I want a strong husband to take care of me. Why on earth should I want good muscle tone?"

Four babies and 20 years later, I suspect she wants all the good muscle tone she can get. We are at the gym-joining age.

Kathy's idea that loving gentleness is tied to weakness rather than strength is probably the idea that underlies much of the reluctance to grant women intellectual, professional, and social power equal to men. In truth, active love is a blending of power and tenderness.

Power means the ability to secure one's way or to achieve one's ends against opposition. That is one of our most basic blessings. Think of a baby's growth in power as he becomes able to grasp objects, to turn over, to crawl, and to walk. The word power comes from an origin meaning "to be able."

A friend of mine yanked irritably at her four-year-old in a store once and told her to quit talking so much. The clerk said quietly, "My own five-year-old has never been able to talk at all. What I would give to hear her pouring out words like your bright little girl."

It takes power to get power, both physically and socially. Some people are born into social power by being born into royalty or wealth. Others achieve social power by using their beauty, brains, bravery, energy, personality, and luck to achieve power resources such as wealth, important friends, or membership in power groups.

In the Old Testament, Prince Jonathan's son became a helpless cripple. But he did not have to be a beggar, because King David took care of him. He had the right connections socially to help with physical weakness.

POWER STEERING

Power is the ability to cause or prevent change. That is why I would like to have power. There are some social changes I would like to prevent (such as oil drilling up and down the coastline) and some social changes I would like to cause (such as stricter enforcement of drunk-driving laws). But there are many more powerful people and industries whose values overrule mine. I feel helpless. Psychologist Rollo May says that when people feel overwhelmed by their lack of power, they resort to violence. Unredeemed powerlessness is painful and destructive.

If I had extreme wealth, I would pour it very carefully into world missions and medical research and food programs and the rescue of children. When I think about those needs I get power-hungry indeed. Power isn't a dirty word to me; it is one of the healthiest words I know.

Of course exploitative and manipulative misuse of power is wrong. But the energy to heal and nurture, the confidence to know and appreciate oneself—these are the powers of a healthy person.

It is true that God's power can become manifest in our weakness. When Corrie ten Boom was a helpless prisoner in a Nazi prison camp, God blessed her in memorable ways. But we have to remember that before the war Corrie had asserted herself by becoming the first licensed woman watchmaker in Holland. The reason she was sent off to a camp was because of her brave and powerful part in the underground movement to save Jews from extermination. And since the war she has ministered powerfully around the world. Corrie ten Boom isn't weak, docile, or passive. She's not pushy and competitive. She is just responsible.

THE BUNNY I ADMIRE MOST

In 1939, one year before the Nazis took over Corrie's homeland, I was a four-year-old country girl, and a children's book came out called *The Country Bunny and the Little Gold Shoes*. When the humble little country girl bunny said, "Someday I shall grow up to be an Easter Bunny—you wait and see!" all the big white rabbits and the jackrabbits with long legs laughed and told her to go eat a carrot. "Leave Easter eggs to great big men bunnies like us." But when Cottontail grew up she was such a good little mother—wise, kind, swift, and clever—that she was indeed chosen to be one of the world's five Easter Bunnies.

And because she had such a loving heart for children (I think of Corrie), she was finally given the hardest task of all—to take the largest, loveliest egg across rivers and mountains to a little cottage on a snowy mountain peak where a very good boy had been sick in bed for a year. She tried so hard to get there on time that she hurt herself. And for her bravery she was given a pair of magic gold shoes which had the power to get her there on time after all.

When I first heard that story and studied the pretty pastel pictures, I hadn't yet heard the real Easter story. That came much later. But even now I don't think the bunnies and eggs and the sick little boy and the golden shoes were all wrong. They were about taking a precious gift to someone in need. And they first taught me the glad news that regardless of a person's size or status or sex, the power of love can lead to the power to serve.

CHAPTER SEVEN

WHOSE LITTLE GIRL ARE YOU?

What Are Today's Options for Grown-up Women?

Ephesians 4: 11-15 (RSV): And his gifts were that some should be apostles, some prophets, some evangelists, some pastors and teachers, to equip the saints for the work of the ministry, for building up the body of Christ, until we all attain to the unity of the faith and of the knowledge of the Son of God, to mature manhood, to the measure of the stature of the fulness of Christ; so that we may no longer be children, tossed to and fro and carried about with every wind of doctrine, by the cunning of men, by their craftiness in deceitful wiles. Rather, speaking the truth in love, we are to grow up in every way into him who is the head, into Christ.

CHAPTER SEVEN

Whose Little Girl Are You?

WHOSE LITTLE GIRL ARE YOU? That is exactly as far as I had gotten on this final chapter of my book when my father suddenly died. I couldn't go on writing for a while.

One weeps like a child when a parent dies. Then one has to act like a grownup and make burial arrangements and comfort others and take care of all the inner and outer business. But the inner child goes on crying part of the time.

My father paid my way through college so that I would be prepared to support myself. (He had to quit school in the eighth grade to go to work and had joined the Navy at 15. No wonder he was thrifty and his main aim was to be a good provider.) Once he asked me if I would be interested in law.

"Good heavens, no!" I had exclaimed, and no more was said. If I had been a boy, I might have done it. But I hoped to remain sweet and feminine, and that seemed totally incompatible with a law career. I can't remember why.

Two or three weeks ago I reminded my father of his fruitless suggestion and finally thanked him for it.

"I think you would have made a good lawyer," he replied simply. That is one of the few direct compliments my father ever gave me, and the last one. It is like a bouquet of roses to me now.

STEREOTYPES THAT HURT

I remember rejecting another person's good advice once simply because I was female. My English teacher, a vivacious unmarried woman of middle years, suggested that in college I should major in English.

"The trouble with majoring in English," I responded, "is that I might end up an old maid English teacher."

We looked at each other aghast and quickly changed the subject. I don't know if she felt sick, but I did. I hope that she realized that she didn't fit the stereotype of an old maid English teacher (who does?), or else I wouldn't have blundered so stupidly.

In contrast, one of the most wounding insults I ever received came in the same school at about the same time. I didn't fit my chemistry teacher's picture of a gifted chemistry student, and so he assumed that I cheated on my tests. He let me hear it by the grapevine. Being shy, I never went to the gruff man and tried to defend myself. There were some brilliant science students in my class, and I felt unworthy to receive scores almost as high as theirs.

That painful experience being my first brush with science, I decided to avoid science classes as much as possible the rest of my life, and that is exactly what I did. Ironically, I learned four years later that my greatest talent was in science all along. After I had majored in English and minored in art in college, nationwide testing showed that I somehow knew more actual science than most of the graduating science majors did. Perhaps it was a bad year for science majors. But even so, my score was absolutely preposterous.

I must have had at least twice as much science ability as the highly respected teacher who thought I was a cheater. I still remember him jabbing at the old Periodic Table and almost shouting at us, "These are all the elements there can be in the universe. This chart is one thing that will never change."

I remember thinking suspiciously, "Time will tell . . ." (It told.) The only other specific statement of his that I remember was that smoking is not harmful to one's health.

In my opinion, we are all fools part of the time, but that's all right. It's part of the human condition.

FLY WITH ME

I never considered science or law or medicine or the ministry for my career simply because I was a girl. I became intensely interested in psychology, but I was advised that the only jobs for women in that field were clerical.

In those days the stylish career for an adventuresome girl was that of an airline stewardess. That is what I wanted to be, but I was a little too short and nearsighted to apply.

From here I can see that my nearsightedness was more inner than outer and that my real lack of stature was in the way I often sold myself short. For example, I didn't object to the fact that I was paid less at college than the boys who did the same work. It struck me as unfair, but I was grateful to get the jobs at all, and so I kept quiet. I worked for seventy-five cents an hour and the boys got eighty-five cents an hour. In those days every dime counted.

I majored in English after all and went on with my love of words and became a teacher. It turned out fine. At least I would rather fly in a poem than in a jet plane any day. I detest the bad air in planes. If I had been three inches taller and had never had eye-wrecking measles, I could have become the unhappiest stylish stewardess who ever flew the friendly skies of United. That was a close call.

WORDS AWAY

Of course females should be free to follow their own true interests and abilities and to receive pay equal to that of males. Many women today think that the traditional English language is full of obstacles to this freedom. One approach to changing old ways of thinking is to change old ways of talking. Some feminists want to smooth out certain eccentricities of English just as real-estate developers in my county bulldoze every grove and hillside they can acquire. (And they have acquired most of them already.)

Last year one leveler illegally destroyed forever a historic natural landmark in our county; it wasn't even on the property he was supposed to be flattening, but it caught his eye because it had an unusual shape. This year a developer bulldozed a huge old tulip tree a mile from my house and put in our ten-thousandth ugly parking lot. That tree, surely worth a small fortune to a landscaper, would have made the man's new shopping center beautiful. But he apparently never looked at it. He was thinking asphalt, not spring beauty. Many language tinkerers also seem to be asphalt-minded.

A couple of weeks ago I heard a radio announcer state seriously, "The onflow of offshore marine air is beginning to be felt in Civic Center." I remember when we called it a sea breeze. A TV announcer kept referring to "extravehicular activity" when he meant "walking on the moon." Some researchers have decided that "greetings mark a transition to increased access, and farewells to a state of decreased access." This means that when you say hello to a person you expect to be with him a while, and when you say good-bye, you don't. In a day when the public at all levels is this tone deaf to language, it is little wonder that feminists have tin ears too.

WHAT'S IN A NAME?

I saw in the paper once that a man from Ecuador named Cesar Enrique Sanchez became an American citizen and changed his name at the same time. What new name did he select? Krzywonski Dennis Savatski. Bless him! I have also read of a young lady who changed her name from Susan Zimbleman to Susan Zimblewoman. I hope she likes it.

But as a Christian I resent someone changing the fine old word chairman into ungainly chairperson. Anyone who believes "In the beginning was the Word, and the Word was with God, and the Word was God . . ." shouldn't treat even our finite words as trash. Words, like nature, are a heritage which we need to enjoy and protect for our children.

Chairman indicates neither gender nor furniture. Rostrum-person or gavel-person would make more sense and be equally ugly.

Man is one of the most beautiful words I have ever heard—a strong poetic word that carries in three letters the weight of centuries of joy and tragedy, hope and despair. One of the basic meanings of man is a person of any age or sex. No one is going to convince me that I am not a man, a full member of mankind, a human, a woman, and, if I can't avoid it, a chairman. (I'll never be the chairperson of anything!)

Word master e. e. cummings wrote a moving poem that began, "pity this busy monster, manunkind . . . ." In my opinion this busy monster will be all the more to be pitied if it becomes personunkind.

I hope that misguided language reformers won't try to change mankind to personkind, man-made to person-made, human to huperson, and woman to woperson. Why don't the reformers turn to professional word lovers for advice? If they distrust men, they could turn to female writers of the stature of novelist Joyce Carol Oates and poet Sylvia Plath. (No, it's too late to ask Sylvia Plath; she gave up and committed suicide.)

THE NAME OF THE JOB

Speaking of suicide, on one of my bad days I borrowed a car which I thought had gears like mine. It didn't, and it had a very grabby clutch besides. When I started to ease out from the alley where I started, the car jumped right out into a line of traffic and stalled. Fortunately, I was not hit broadside because the car that I jumped in front of was being very carefully driven. It was a police car.

Try as I might, I couldn't back out of the way, because I couldn't find reverse gear. So I had to pull the rest of the way out onto the street and be escorted to a nearby parking lot in ignominy. When the policeman asked for my driver's license, she turned out to be a lovely young woman. I will always be grateful to her for her kind understanding (she couldn't find the reverse gear either), her stern official written warning, and her decision not to give me a ticket. We can use more police officers like that one.

That same difficult week I had to place a collect call to my husband. To my surprise, the long-distance operator was a man. He asked me who he should say was calling. "I'm his wife," I answered awkwardly.

"OK, I'll tell him the boss is on the line." Then he bantered with me the whole time as he put the call through. He didn't know that I was going through some personal sadness and that he warmed me like sunshine. We can use more telephone operators like that one.

Now at my grocery store I find that most of the "box boys" are girls. Of course the "box boys" have always used bags. "Bag girls"? I asked one of the girls what her title is. "Checker's helper," she answered, as if I should have known. It's hard to keep up. (I still say TV station instead of channel sometimes.)

Changing box boy to checker's helper and fireman to firefighter seem all right to me. (My three-year-old son planned to become a fireman until he learned that they didn't go around setting fires all day.) But some of the occupational convolutions we face today such as design technicians for draftsmen, cargo handlers for longshoremen, camera operators for cameramen, dining room servers for waiters and waitresses, sewing workers instead of seamstresses, and sales representatives in place of salesmen seem to me like sad little jokes about equal opportunity rather than part of the real thing.

RIDDLE ME THIS

When I was a child I heard the old church riddle, "Why do we say amen instead of awomen after our prayers?" The answer was "Because we sing hymns, not hers." I thought it was delightfully corny then. I wouldn't have believed it possible that 30 years later someone would suggest changing hurricanes to themicanes so that they could have male names as well as female names. I saw it, but I still can't believe it.

In English we have long used he, him, and his to refer to a person of either sex. "Each student opened his desk" has always been neutral and correct unless every single student was definitely female. It worked so easily until now. Only people who didn't know correct grammar would say, "Each student opened their desk." Now I have read an entire bestselling book intentionally written that way! It sounded terrible in print. The reason for the switch is that some people are suddenly up in arms against the unisex nature of he, him, and his.

"A person should wash his hands before eating" strikes them as an insult to women.

Some defenders of the word "their" have come up with several newly invented pronouns which could serve sexlessly in place of "his." We could say, "Each student opened hisher desk," or "Each student opened es desk." You think it couldn't happen?

A recent national opinion poll showed that 14 percent of the women surveyed prefer the recent invention Ms. instead of Miss or Mrs. That's a lot of women! If the person who invented Ms. had a patent on it, he or she would be rich today. (How does he or she grab you? Yech.)

WHAT ARE WOMEN ENTITLED TO?

Miss and Mrs. are both abbreviated forms of the old title Mistress (remember "Mistress Mary, quite contrary, how does your garden grow?"), and Mistress was used for either single or married women. Ms., although a new invention, follows naturally in that old tradition as a new abbreviation of the same old neutral term that gave us Miss and Mrs.

There is nothing sinister or disrespectful about the non-commital Ms. It is short, polite, and practical and will save the nation much ink, time, and energy. (Of course, we would save more ink, time, and energy if we followed the example of the old Quakers and dropped the whole silly title business altogether.) The only disadvantage to Ms. is that it looks better than it sounds. Try reading my limerick aloud. (This limerick is having fun with abbreviations rather than making fun of feminists.)

Gee Whs.!
A thirsty young lady named Ls.
Was a libber and called herself Ms.
    She drank a whole pail
    Of ice-cold ginger ale
And said, "How I do like its fs."

Of course the adoption of Ms. is a minor matter compared to the trend for some women to retain their birth-given names when they marry rather than taking their husbands' names. Women who are public figures have done that all along, but rarely have ordinary women tried it until now. It is legal in most states. It will make record-keeping more difficult, I suppose, but the real puzzler is how to name the children. So far, couples are handling this in various interesting ways.

Christians who see the matter of names as a moral issue should remember that our present system of married surnames only dates back to the Middle Ages. The early church didn't dream of such a strange custom. And Iceland has never yet adopted our system. There a husband, wife, and baby all have different last names. It doesn't diminish their love and loyalty at all.

WEAKER AND WEAKER SEX

Not that any country today has a surplus of family love and loyalty. In America there seems to be some confusion between being free and being cheap. When some people use the term "liberated woman" they mean a woman who is ruled by whim rather than by wisdom, by infatuation rather than by dedication, or by selfishness rather than by common sense. Some liberation. It makes a lot of money for some women's magazines.

Women have never really had a corner on purity, but today they are being congratulated by certain businessmen with a vested interest because they've come a long way, baby. All the way to the lung-cancer ward. Other signs of being grown up and free include alcoholism, adultery, abortion, easy divorce, and venereal disease. Lung cancer is indeed a new accomplishment for women, but the other items have been around a long time, baby.

I heard a married couple on the radio once promoting a book about swinging and swapping. The wife's gentle voice lowered modestly as she admitted that her false guilt about their unconventional sex life (the words adultery and fornication were carefully avoided) had forced them to go to a psychologist. The helpful psychologist, in turn, had chosen them as the subject of his book about emancipated marriages.

"You see," the husband explained, "people have never really been monogamous. But I'm afraid," he said, his voice dropping to a somber tone, "the Church has indoctrinated us against the sexual variety we crave." He went on to explain that the guilty Church has thus promoted cheating and dishonesty in marriage.

"Cheating and dishonesty are very bad!" he continued. Frank, open sexual experimentation and multiple love affairs are honest and healthy.

Although he praised honesty, he lacked enough of it to admit that the largest nation in the world, strictly atheistic and anti-Christian, is chaste and monogamous today. In fact, Red China is said to have thus conquered venereal disease, which is a plague in the United States. I guess VD is supposed to be a healthy kind of ailment.

What struck me most strongly was the obvious fact that dishonesty is even more natural to the human race than marital infidelity; it starts much earlier and lasts longer. Apparently it has not yet occurred to the liberated husband that his hang-up about honesty is an unnatural attitude (notice my somber tone) unfortunately brought about by years of Church indoctrination.

FREE LOVE

I remember reading in a popular sex manual apparently written for undersexed women of medium-low IQ (fill your bathtub with Jello) that the only restrictions on sex affairs for women today are: (1) Don't steal your own sister's husband, and (2) Don't have affairs with Lesbians. I think orgies were left optional as a matter of taste. Since the author threw out all morals and scruples and recommended pure self-gratification as life's only value, I was surprised that she was so narrow-minded about brothers-in-law and homosexuality. It struck me as pure prudishness on her part, once love, truth, and ethics were tossed away. If I were a brother-in-law or a Lesbian, I would be deeply offended.

Many women are looking more for personal freedom and economic freedom than for sexual freedom. I know the ironic case of one frustrated woman who felt oppressed and left her husband and family after 30 years to get a job and start dating. Her job was terrible and immediately gave her ulcers, and then her ex-husband learned that he stood to inherit almost $100,000 out of the blue. The emancipated woman, of course, didn't get a penny, and ended up going to work for her aged father.

Some people can't win for losing. But let's face it. In the long run, who really can?

A young man who asked an uninterested girl for a date was told, "I'll be free the second Tuesday of next week." Realistically, that is the only day when any woman (or man) will be totally free. And love will be free. I refer to the fact that for a Christian there is an incredible week coming sometime which will have two Tuesdays, or two million Tuesdays, and every day will be as a thousand years.

In the meantime, we just have to choose what yoke we are willing to bear—if we are given any choice. And be thankful if we find that yoke easy and the burden light.

LADY BE GOOD

John Calvin said, "Does a person demand his rights? Certainly, I am prepared to grant him his rights, but in so doing I shall say that he has no other rights than to fulfill his duties."

I have been thinking about that claim for some time, and so far I can't think of any women's rights which are not also their duties. Perhaps there are some. But I think of a woman's right to provide for her own needs and those of her dependents. I think of her right to influence herself and the world for good. I think of her right to be a creative, original, realistic person absorbed in life and growth, making full use of her potentialities. I think of her right to love and be loved, to respect and be respected.

Calvin and I aren't referring to questionable legal rights such as the right to own slaves or the right to drink yourself to death or the right to withhold love from babies or to waste food. We are talking about the moral rights that the women's movement is demanding. The rights of full personhood.

Women (and men) haven't always been granted those rights, and even when they have received them, they haven't always exercised them. That's when rights unclaimed become duties unfulfilled.

LIVING DOLLS

Under the skin of most grown-up American women there is a little girl, and that's good. That is where certain tears come from, and laughter. That's the source of spontaneous caring and acting. It is a source of awe and delight and playfulness. Pity the adult with no healthy child inside.

But big parts of our society like to see American women as living Barbie dolls rather than real women. Barbie dolls are good for business because they have expensive tastes and no brains or hearts. They have no bothersome ideas about issues like the dangerous hormones that are injected into beef in the United States, and every one of them exists stiffly for her possessions. You see lots of them in magazines and on television.

Barbie's possessions include a blankly handsome male doll named Ken and a lavish wardrobe and recreational equipment. Barbie doesn't know or care that $10.00 can buy enough vaccine to protect 1,250 poor children from TB.

I heard of a Barbie-type wife who promised to stop smoking if her husband would buy her a pair of diamond earrings. Once she got the earrings she started to smoke again. She in-

Whose Little Girl Are You?

creases the gross national product twice that way, by supporting both the jewelry business and the tobacco industry. American advertising just loves Barbie-doll women. American women are the consumers of the world. They are able to fill their lives buying and using and caring for things. (You have to fill your life with something.)

William Wordsworth summed up the Barbie-doll life:

> The world is too much with us: late and soon,
> Getting and spending, we lay waste our powers.

Getting and spending is a major way in which women ward off the fear of meaninglessness and the fear of death. I know of better ways.

PRESCRIPTION FOR MEANING

I had just met a soft bright woman in my neighborhood drugstore. She was the pharmacist's wife and liked to work with him. As I waited for my prescription, I discovered that the next day a foster child was coming to their home.

"We'll have a baby in a year or two," she confided, "but there is no hurry, and in the meantime we have an extra room and there are so many children who need help. This nine-year-old girl has been in seven foster homes in the past two years. She doesn't know how to feel love deeply anymore. We will keep her until someone wants to adopt her. Not many people will adopt a child that old."

This woman used to be an inner-city teacher. She knew disturbed children and cherished them.

"Will you go on working here with your husband and hire a sitter?" I asked.

"Oh, no," she replied. "This is my last day at work with him. I'll stay home now. We'll do all we can for her."

There was joy almost shining over the counter between us. As I left, she asked simply. "Will you pray for me?"

FAT COWS

This young woman reminds me of what Amos longed for when he became furious at the rich women in Samaria and tore into them as recorded in Amos 4. For my own personal admonition I loosely paraphrase *The Living Bible*. I don't think Amos would mind.

> Listen to me, you fat cows of Bashan living in America—you women who encourage Congress to vote against the poor while you ignore collections for the needy—you who never have enough to wear! The Lord God has sworn by his holiness that the time will come when he will put hooks in your noses and lead you away like the cattle you are; they will force the last of you away with electric cattle prods! You will be hauled from your beautiful homes and tossed onto the center divider of the nearest freeway. The Lord has said it.

Then I like to go on to Amos 5:

> Be good and flee evil and live! Then Jesus will truly be your Helper, as you have claimed he is . . . . Away with your poems of praise and your Christian books—they are mere noise to my ears. I will not read your articles, no matter how good the scholarship is. I want to see a mighty flood of justice—a torrent of doing good.

Thank you, Amos. I need that once in a while.

HARD-HEADED WOMEN

The world seems full of hard-hearted, soft-headed people. What we need is soft-hearted, hard-headed women. Compassion with capability. (A hard-headed woman is one who is stubborn, strong-willed, and practical.) Then perhaps God could see His mighty flood of justice—a torrent of doing good.

Charles Williams said once, "No one can paddle his own canoe, but we can all paddle someone else's." I think he was talking about prayer and spiritual support. I would like to see us all paddling each other's canoes socially, too.

Ideally, men, being strongest, would protect the nation's women from all kinds of rape, low self-esteem, exploitation, discrimination, and uselessness. Then women could actively protect the nation's children from poverty, cruelty, malnutrition, corruption, and injustice.

But it is a fact of history that not enough men have had the strength and understanding to protect and enable women in the first place. That is why women have had to struggle so hard on their own behalf. Pity the children, who are always at the bottom of the heap in America. It makes me angry. (Seven foster homes in two years!)

Simone Weil was a soft-hearted, hard-headed woman if there ever was one. Born to Jewish parents in France in 1909, she cared passionately about the poor and underprivileged. She was active in social causes and taught high school in her twenties, but she had to quit because of frail health. At about 30 she began studying both the Bible and Hindu scriptures, and she became convinced that Christ on the cross was a bridge between God and man. She died a Christian at 32. She is remembered as an outstanding philosopher and mystic.

Simone Weil said serenely about injustice (which she hated as much as any of us), "Men owe us what we imagine they will give us. We must forgive them this debt."

FORGIVE MEN THEIR DEBTS

I have a close friend whose husband of 20 years recently walked out on her for a younger woman and took all their hard-won financial security and their plans for a comfortable retirement with him. She had neither the health nor training for a good job; she had been a full-time wife and mother all those years. (I remember how at the beginning she had to wash diapers by hand, they were so poor.) She always was a devoted and submissive wife. At first she was wild with grief, but then a wise minister-counselor saved her from nervous collapse. He showed her Weil's wisdom, "We must forgive," and helped her to do it. She knew her husband was treating her dreadfully, but she let her anger go; his sin wasn't really her problem. She very soon found a whole new life, untinged with bitterness. God quickly and completely healed her broken heart. Her happy Christian attitude was most disconcerting to her husband during the divorce proceedings; it seemed to hurt his ego. (He is now married to a hellcat, which serves him right for a while.)

Of course women have been treated unfairly in our society in many ways. (Not only is the median income of full-time female workers vastly lower than that for males, but the difference has increased a lot in recent years!) Nevertheless, in women's just struggle for power, the healthy power that Simone Weil urged upon us is still free for the taking—the power of forgiveness.

My grandmother was a wonderfully kind and gentle woman who endured a hard and unfair life. All she needed was for a car to jump the curb and run her down on the sidewalk and leave her limping in pain her last years. When the driver wouldn't even do so much as pay her doctor bill, she just forgave him. That was her way. I was a little girl and she smiled quiet blessings on me, and her white hair was like a halo. Kindness shone in all her wrinkles, and her lap was full of serenity.

THE BEST OF THINGS

I read a stern rule once: Never say or think, "If only . . . ." I tried the rule, and it has proved invaluable. It is a way of forgiving life for things that went wrong. According to Carl Jung, an individuated person is one who finds out how to make the best of things. That sounds trite, but when you see it work in someone like my grandmother, it is awesome. It somehow reminds me of the old campfire song:

> From the hills I gather courage,
> Vision of a day to be;
> Strength to lead and faith to follow,
> All are given unto me.

Injustice is a terrible thing, and fighting injustice is our Christian duty and costly joy. But suffering injustice is not the worst fate. (Causing it is.) Paul's old words ring new to me every day: "Moreover we know that to those who love God, who are called according to his plan, everything that happens fits into a pattern for good" (Rom. 8: 28, Phillips).

Ugo Betti, an Italian playwright, said it this way: "To believe in God is to know that all the rules will be fair and that there will be wonderful surprises."

All I can say to that is: Maranatha! Come, Lord Jesus.